Impractical GRACE

Impractical GRACE

JOHN S. BUSHMAN

CFI
SPRINGVILLE, UTAH

This is not an official publication of The Church of Jesus Christ of Latter-day Saints. The opinions and views expressed herein belong solely to the author and do not necessarily represent the opinions or views of Cedar Fort, Inc. Permission for the use of sources, graphics, and photos is also solely the responsibility of the author.

This is a work of fiction. The characters, names, incidents, places, and dialogue are products of the author's imagination, and are not to be construed as real.

ISBN 13: 978-1-59955-475-4

Published by CFI, an imprint of Cedar Fort, Inc., 2373 W. 700 S., Springville, UT 84663
Distributed by Cedar Fort, Inc., www.cedarfort.com

LIBRARY OF CONGRESS CATALOGING-IN-PUBLICATION DATA

Bushman, John S. (John Stanford), 1971-
Impractical grace / John S. Bushman.
p. cm.
ISBN 978-1-59955-475-4
1. Marriage--Religious aspects--Church of Jesus Christ of Latter-day Saints. 2. Grace (Theology) 3. Christian life--Mormon authors. I. Title.

BX8641.B87 2011
248.8'44--dc22

2010035118

Cover design by Danie Romrell
Cover design © 2011 by Lyle Mortimer
Edited and typeset by Kelley Konzak

Printed in the United States of America

10 9 8 7 6 5 4 3 2 1

Printed on acid-free paper

PRAISE FOR *IMPRACTICAL GRACE*

"John Bushman takes a fresh look at the concept of grace, a belief we sometimes overlook but that is eternally significant. Following the struggles of his characters and witnessing the healing they receive after their application and understanding of grace is heartwarming and inspiring. I look forward to sharing this book with friends and loved ones, especially those that continue to fight through the battles of life."

—Don Spangler, Texas

"This book has helped me in a remarkable way to understand the doctrine of the Lord's grace and the enabling power offered to me through His Atonement. As I read this book, I felt a sense of comfort and peace and realized that I too, like the characters in the book, can receive the divine help the Savior offers to lift me and draw me to seek aid through the healing power of the Atonement. I especially love how the author offers practical everyday application, backed with scriptural quotes, in a simple yet profound approach! I have read this book twice, yet I know I will revisit it again to feel once more the serenity that the Savior's grace can give to me for my life."

—Beverly Smith, California

TO TINA,
TORI, EMILY, NATALIE,
JOSHUA, AND JORDAN.
THANK YOU FOR THE GRACE AND
GOODNESS YOU HAVE SHOWN ME.

contents

acknowledgments

This book has been spread out over quite a few years, so I need to thank my whole family for their great patience with me. I also need to thank my dear wife, Tina, for seeing my blind spots and for her keen insights. This would be a very different book if it were not for her suggestions and being a great sounding board for my thoughts and ideas. There are many others who have edited and helped me in the process, such as Don Spangler, Ruth Baird, Beverly Smith, Irene Olsen, Nettie Francis, and too many more to mention here. I am also very thankful for the wonderful people at Cedar Fort, including Kelley Konzak, Jennifer Fielding, Danie Romrell, and Emily Showgren.

It is my desire that this book share powerful insights to the Lord's grace and love while delivering those insights in an interesting story. But by using this method, I have found it difficult to share every supporting quote or scripture. This is why a bit of additional information is found at the end of each chapter.

The characters in this book are fictional, and any similarities or resemblance is coincidental. As with most books by members of the Church, neither I nor this book has any authority to speak for The Church of Jesus Christ of Latter-day Saints.

chapter one

KEN AND DEBORAH: A YEAR AGO

As Ken Richards drove home from work on that August evening, he considered the good life he had created for himself. Ken had worked hard, encouraged his three children, served in the Church, and been a good husband to his wife, Deborah. Since law school Ken had built a solid and respected legal practice in their town. From the time he was a teenager, he wanted to be a lawyer. The superhero appeal of righting the world of injustice always stirred deep in his soul. And so he did just that. Ken was a great lawyer because he loved his work of trying to make the world right.

At quarter to seven, he pulled up in his driveway as the sun was setting behind a golden red sunset.

"Sorry I'm a bit late again," Ken said as he came through the family room, where Deborah sat at the computer.

"That's fine, honey," Deborah said. "I'm just finishing an email, and dinner won't be ready for a few minutes."

"Where're the kids?"

"The girls are playing in their room, and Jimmy just went into the kitchen."

Ken went into the kitchen, where he could smell the lasagna cooking in the top oven but saw that Deborah had forgotten to put in the French bread she had bought to warm in the other oven. *I'll get it going,* Ken thought.

"Hey, come here, Jimmy," Ken called in a voice that usually brought their five-year-old running in excitement. Often the running hug that came would quickly turn into the two wrestling and laughing together.

"Deborah, where's Jimmy?"

"Check in the backyard, he needs to come in," Deborah called back as she stood from the computer to go into the kitchen.

"Jimmy," Ken said in a louder but more concerned voice as he walked onto the deck in the yard. Ken started to walk to the side yard when he caught a scene in his side vision that made his blood chill. The gate to the pool was cracked open.

"Jimmy!" Ken now shouted with panic flowing as he ran to the pool. There he saw the sum of every parent's fear—his son, face down in the water. Immediately a blur of action and feelings screamed into motion. In that moment, everything in life changed.

chapter two

ANNA AND MITCH: TWO WEEKS AGO

The reflection in the mirrors looked different now. Anna stood remembering her wedding day six years ago, when the temple sealer asked the two of them to stand next to each other in the reflection of two enormous mirrors that were hung to face each other. Her long red hair was pulled up and curled with a few strands hanging down, accenting her porcelain skin and dark brown eyes. She and Mitch beamed with the joy and excitement of starting their new lives together as husband and wife.

As they looked at each other in the mirror in front of them, they saw their reflection repeated continuously through a visual corridor. The sealer said the repeating images represented eternal marriage and how their relationship could last forever. Anna remembered tears in Mitch's eyes and him holding her closer as they looked on together. That moment remained a snapshot in her mind. She had felt so much love for him.

But now, six years later, Anna strangely could not recall exactly what that love felt like. Anna stood alone in the empty sealing room, just off of the celestial room, after the ward temple night. Again she saw the giant mirrors facing each other. But this time the impressions they gave her were considerably different. As she looked down the passageway of the repeating mirror images, her excitement was replaced with quiet revulsion. Although the sealing room was bright and beautiful, each time she was replicated in the mirror she saw herself becoming increasingly small. Not only that, but each new image of her bled out more color and left her in increasingly dark shades of green and gray.

It felt to Anna that the mirrors represented the brightness of who she once was, what she had become, and who she would be. The forecasted future of her life married to Mitch looked awful. Like the images, she felt that she was becoming a smaller person. She now didn't like the person she saw in the mirror like she once did. In the years prior to marriage, Anna had grown immensely as a single adult and enjoyed who she had become. She was happy and enthusiastic. She felt like marriage would continue to bring out the best in her. But it hadn't. Instead it seemed to have brought out the worst.

As Anna continued looking through the mirrors, she saw the years stretching forward. Anna was still beautiful, with her straight red hair falling on her shoulders and her light skin. But the quick smile she once had was gone. Now her face seemed to reflect the weight of her failing marriage. Strangely, no matter how she moved in the mirrors, her image didn't continue on. Either the mirrors seemed to end as they gradually turned a corner, or her own image would be in the way, preventing her from seeing further.

Standing alone, Anna thought about the temple recommend interview she'd had last month with her bishop. "Is there anything in your conduct relating to members of your family that is not in harmony with the teachings of the Church?" *Does despising your husband count?* Anna now thought. When the question was asked, she had quickly answered no, considering the question to be asking about the most grievous of sins. But now, because of her marriage, she wondered if she was even worthy to be in the temple. Would loathing your spouse be grounds for not receiving a temple recommend? Had she lied to the bishop?

It amazed Anna how differently she had seen things before. When Mitch and Anna met, she was so impressed with his strong features and striking personality. In college she made the most of her interest in math and science by becoming an engineering student. This immediately put her in the study company of many guys who had similar majors, and all were impressed with her unique talents. Most of the guys who had taken Anna on dates came from her class associations.

Mitch had a different background. With almost unnaturally broad shoulders and natural ability, he was the sports hero in high school. He could joke, tease, and have his way in almost every situation. After high school and his mission, he saw that popularity didn't matter like it once did. Where in high school, it was practically predestined who he was to date and how the girl must look, now he loved that he was open to like and date whoever he chose.

As Mitch studied in the library one day, Anna (the girl surrounded and pampered by handfuls of guys) caught his eye. Even at a distance, everything about her started to command his attention. After watching her for a couple of weeks in this way, he determined that he would charm and start dating her. Anna was soon swept off her feet. Both were fascinated by the other.

Did we marry too quickly? Anna thought, looking into the big mirrors. *If we didn't take things so fast, I'm sure I would have seen what he was really like.* Mitch was one to joke more than Anna. As they dated his joking was usually in fun, but she saw that sometimes he could be cruel in his sarcastic way. Marriage didn't make it better. Anna's way of dealing with his meanness was the silent treatment. In the first years of their marriage, he would apologize. Later he learned that he could just do something nice, and talk as though nothing had happened. Although this got them talking to each other sooner, injuries didn't heal, and the scar tissue started to build up.

Anna had a much stronger personality than the swooning girls Mitch once knew. At first, Mitch was attracted to her forcefulness and her keen intellect. She was intelligent and could help you see that. Nothing was wrong with that until Mitch and Anna began to disagree more often.

Anna would have ended the marriage years earlier if it weren't for their daughter, Caitlin. Anna and Mitch were good parents to their daughter, but after a few years, no effort was made with each other. Growing up, she had seen what divorce had done to her friends, and she didn't want to put her daughter through the same.

I can't live like this forever. Don't I deserve a little better? Anna thought as she continued to look through the mirrors in the increasing haze of future years.

chapter three

ERICA: SEVEN YEARS AGO

"Dear God, no," Erica pled with clenched fists.

Erica sat on her bed, rocking back and forth with her knees pulled closely to her in a fetal position. The room was dark except for small slits of moonlight falling onto her bed from the aluminum window blinds above her head.

"Please," Erica started again in prayer as she rolled open her blinds and looked up into the heavens at the almost blinding full moon. "I can't do this. Help me." Erica was just twelve years old. About a year earlier, she and her mom had been in a bad situation with bills, and it looked like they were going to lose their home. Then as if in answer to prayer, Dean came into her mother's life, and they married a short time later. It seemed he was the solution to all of their needs for a time. But a few months into the marriage, he began to touch Erica in uncomfortable ways. At first she told herself it was just affection like some parents have for their children. But slowly it grew worse. When Erica started to resist, Dean rationalized his behavior, which slowly turned to coercion. He threatened that if she talked about it to anyone, he would make her and her mom homeless. They had nowhere they could go. Erica's stomach twisted as she thought of things he would do to her. She couldn't live like this.

"Please, please God. Make it stop," Erica begged as she looked up and prayed. She now scooted and adjusted the blinds so she could be completely bathed in the moonlight shining onto her bed. As Erica continued to pray, she looked from the moon to the well-manicured neighbor's yards and houses all around. She wondered if the happy perfect families inside could possibly imagine the private nightmare she was going through just a short distance away.

"You can do anything," Erica pled as she looked back into the sky. "Please make it stop," she said as a feeling of hope started to grow in her.

Erica suddenly flinched as she heard her stepfather's car door shut in the driveway. Her mom was working late as she did each Wednesday night. Erica knew again that there would be no one there to protect her. She slowly and thoughtfully moved out of the light and rolled the blinds closed again in the darkness.

chapter four

STUART AND EDEN NORTH: PRESENT DAY

Eden came quietly into their study and placed her hands on her husband's shoulders, rubbing gently. "Are you doing okay, Stu?" Eden asked. Bishop Stuart North folded down the list of names in his hand.

"I'm okay," he spoke and signed back to her. Then he placed his hand on his wife's and looked into her eyes in a kind, reassuring way. The Norths had been married for twenty-five years when Eden started to develop hearing problems along with her common headaches. After months of doctor appointments and tests, a tumor was discovered in her lower brain stem. Within weeks she could no longer hear despite the removal of the tumor. Eden and Stuart then began the journey of learning to communicate again. Both had to learn sign language. Stu had to learn to communicate by signing and writing out messages while Eden had to learn to sign in order to understand what he was communicating. She was surprised at how well she could read people's lips when they talked. Even though Eden could no longer hear, she could still speak; yet the tone and modulation in her voice was slowly beginning to change. Now it had been four years since Eden's hearing loss, and the two had long gotten used to their new communication style. Perhaps they communicated just as well now as they once did. By this point in their lives, two of their children had already left home. The oldest was married, and the second was just returning from a mission and starting school. But their last child, Julie, still lived at home, being in high school, and she'd learned sign language as well.

"Come to bed Stu," Eden said, dragging her fingers through the back of his thick, black, graying hair. "You can't change the world in a single night." Eden was beautiful, with her thick, curly hair and happy face. Although gray was starting to mix into her hair also, it wasn't only her hair that made her so beautiful. It was how her eyes came alive every time she smiled. Although she had worn glasses for as long as Stuart knew her, the glasses never got in the way of the energy in her eyes.

Stuart nodded with a kind smile. "I just wish I could do something to help these people," he signed back. Eden could see in his eyes that he was carrying a heavy burden. Two months ago, Stuart North had been called to be the bishop of the Lake Crescent Ward. Stuart was the most surprised by the call. He had served the Young Men there for as long as they had been in the ward and had blessed those young men's lives. He had a soft-spoken, quiet nature about him, and people knew him to be a wise and caring man. It was apparent that he cared by how he spoke and concerned himself with others' needs before his own.

Although he'd served with the Young Men for the last ten years, Brother North thought he knew the ward and its members pretty well. But within the first week of being called to be the bishop, he felt like he had to constantly keep his jaw from dropping in surprise when he would hear of the various troubles different families were having. He was surprised to learn of how many in his ward struggled with marital problems, addictions, financial chaos, and other pains and difficulties.

"I'm not sure how I can ever really be a 'judge in Israel' for these people," Stuart signed as he spoke. "I'm the last person that should be judging anyone."

"That's good dear," Eden said. "That's just the kind of mercy I would hope God would have with all of us."

Bishop North was a complicated man. His past had shaped him differently from the mold of most men. His childhood was cruel, which led him later to hate—not just the few who had hurt him, but also hate God and every other person in the world. His heart had been broken young and had become cold in anger.

Then a stranger saved him. Someone who had nothing to gain from him. That man's care and love challenged all Stuart had grown to feel for the world. The man was a messenger of

God's divine love, and that love evaporated the hate in his soul and changed everything in him.

Because of his serious nature, strangers would sometimes observe and wonder if Stuart had not truly forgiven himself. But those close to him saw a man right with God. A man who despised the evil that once held his heart. A man determined to now serve the Lord and Master of his life. With Stuart's forgiveness came his servitude and the careful servant's mind toward God, which ruled Stuart with consistency.

Though God remembers sin no more, Stuart's memories of his past never really left him. Although forgiven, he felt a detached shame of what he once was. It shaped Stuart North into becoming a quiet and unassuming person. Humbled by the evil that was once in him, he was now broken and deferred to God.

"What do you hope to do tonight?" Eden asked kindly as she sat in a chair facing her husband and looked into his tired eyes.

"I don't know," Stuart shrugged as he spoke and signed. "I'm honestly surprised that people who have had the gospel their whole lives would have so many problems like these."

"The gospel doesn't make it so people won't have problems," Eden corrected. "Everyone will have storms in life. The gospel is what helps us get through the storms." As bishop, Eden's husband never told her things given to him in confidence. Even though Eden didn't know all the particulars of the ward members' lives, she did have a general idea of who in the ward was struggling.

"You're right," Stuart signed, looking deeply into her eyes, "but these people aren't getting through their storms." There she saw a discouragement that frightened her a bit. "Eden, they're going down in the storm. They're sinking and drowning. The real essences of these members' problems are not the random tragedies that happen in this world. The real problem is how they are dealing with the troubles. It's like they're missing the parts of the gospel that keep people afloat in the difficult times."

Silence seemed to emphasize his point until Eden pulled her chair closer to his. She leaned forward, swiveled his chair to face her, and then took his face in her hands and looked deeply into his eyes as if to read something in them. Then Eden smiled mischievously and began to look at other areas of his face as if pretending to inspect his personal grooming skills. "You keep praying for those people Stu, and God is going to help you know how to bless them," Eden said as she redirected her gaze in his eyes with her playful smile. "Seriously."

The pickup truck rolled to a stop on the side of the highway. *I can't believe this*, Stuart thought as he pulled the hood release below the steering wheel.

Last week Stuart had found the perfect vehicle to give his son while he was going to school at Central Washington University. The truck needed a little fixing up, but it wasn't anything Stuart hadn't learned long ago how to fix himself. Besides, he'd gotten the truck for fifteen hundred dollars. Early that Saturday morning Stuart had been fixing the truck to get it ready for the two-hour drive to the university. But now Stuart looked under the hood, down beside the engine, to see that the serpentine belt had broken.

"Need a little help?" an older gentleman asked, walking up to the truck.

"I think so," Stuart replied. "Thanks for stopping. I think it overheated from a broken belt. On a truck like this, I'm not going to be able to fix this out here. I think I'll need a tow truck, and I don't have my phone with me."

"We don't live far from here, and I know just the guy to tow you in," the man said.

"That would be great," Stuart said as he leaned from the side of the truck to see the man's wife in the passenger seat of an '85 Buick wave back to him. "I would really appreciate it."

"Sit tight," the man said as he started to walk back to his car. "You'll have a tow truck here in just a little while." Stuart North started to feel bad when he saw the car turning around to go the other way; he was making this older couple change their plans just to help him.

After a half hour, a tow truck came, driven by a gruff, portly man.

"Thanks for coming," Stuart said.

"That's my job," the man replied, hardly looking at him.

"Is it okay if I ask how much it's going to be?" Stu asked as the man started to look under the pickup truck.

"The best price you've ever gotten," the man said, almost ignoring Stuart as he worked. "It's been taken care of."

"What do you mean?" Stu asked with surprise.

"The old man and woman you met already paid me to tow you into town," the tow truck driver said as he walked to his truck to back it up to the pickup. Feeling embarrassed, Stu looked down at his work clothes and the older truck. He realized he looked far more needy than he actually was.

"I think the older man got the wrong idea," Stu said as the man started to hook up the truck. "I can pay for this. I'll pay for it and you go give that man his money back," Stu said, opening his wallet.

"Can't do that," the man said, continuing to work. "He would never speak to me again if I did. Just put your wallet back in your pocket, get in the truck, and I'll take you into town."

"I can't let him do that. I really can pay for it," Stuart began again.

"That's dumb," the man said indignantly. "You can't let someone just be kind to you?"

"No, it's just—"

"First time someone's been kind to you?" the man asked as he opened his door.

"No."

"Then how about you just let him be kind to you, and I'll tell him you were grateful."

"Yes, of course," Stuart replied. "But why don't you give me his name so—"

"You just don't get it, do you?" the driver said. "Just be grateful."

Stuart slowly nodded his head. "Then please do tell him thank you for me."

"I will," the man said with the smallest hint of a smile.

On the drive into town, Bishop North reflected on his feelings. He thought about why it was so hard to receive the old man's generosity. He wondered why he was already thinking of someone in need he might be able to help. Then flashes of realization started to come to him. It was as if, through this experience, the Lord was trying to teach him how to help those ward members on his list. Stuart pulled out his notebook and began writing down impressions and scriptures that came to mind. It wasn't all together yet, but he was pretty sure he now knew the path the Lord wanted him to take with a few of the members in his ward. He realized that almost all of the people on his list were missing a particular gospel principle.

Bishop North looked out the window with a simple smile. He smiled in the realization that the very love that the older couple had demonstrated was the love these people in his ward needed to learn about and show. The ideas now flowed to his mind as he thought of these ward members whose struggles had weighed his thoughts. In his planning he found himself thanking the Lord with a heart overflowing. He now knew what to do.

He also wrote a thank-you note to the old man and a second one for the tow truck driver and left them both on the seat of the tow truck.

chapter five

THE INVITATION

Bishop Stuart North was an extraordinary small business owner. On his mission in the Philippines, he was exposed to real bread for the first time. Not the kind of fluffy nothing you get in the grocery store but real bread with substance. While on his mission, every morning at seven, and afternoon at three, the bakeries would put their bread out to cool from baking. The young Elder North found the smell intoxicating and was hooked. While in college he dreamed of owning his own bakery and sandwich shop and studied and worked with that goal in mind. His studies were in how to own a small business. For his part-time jobs, he would hop from different grocery stores and bakeries to any other place that baked. He was becoming a master.

Now Stuart North owned one of the most popular establishments in the town's large shopping center. Learning his marketing skills from his mission, he used the same technique. He figured out a way to cool his bread by venting out the incredible aroma to those who passed by. A small sniff and most would be hooked. Then Stuart would finish them off by offering large samples of one of the different breads, slathered in real butter. Though his bread was quite a bit more expensive than the bread from the grocery store, he had gained a large clientele of regular customers. Also, his bakery became famous for lunchtime sandwiches using the heavenly bread.

Erica, now nineteen years old, was one of those who became hooked. So much so that she became one of Stuart North's favorite employees. Erica's life had been tragic. Five years earlier, her stepfather had been arrested and sent to jail. Erica and her mother had struggled, and Erica had dropped out of high school. Getting hints of her situation, Stuart North looked out for her and tried to help where he could. In many ways, he felt a kinship with her because of her struggles and his own background.

Bread wasn't the only draw of the job. She respected Mr. North immensely. Needless to say, there were few proper male figures in her life, but Stuart North was kind and fair. She knew he cared. When Stuart's wife, Eden, would come into the shop, she would often invite Erica to dinner, which she always declined. She would have loved to go, but she was afraid to trust people too much. Besides, there was also part of her that was afraid that if she observed Mr. North too closely, she would see that he wasn't as great of a man as she had concluded over the last couple of years working with him.

Working for Stuart North was one of the only good things that had happened in Erica's life. It also seemed to be the only source of personal satisfaction for her. She worked hard to do everything just right, perhaps the only thing in her life that she worked hard at. If someone asked her what she wanted to do with her life, she would tell them she wanted to maybe one day own a bakery of her own. But if the truth were known, she couldn't imagine working anywhere except for Stuart North.

One day when now-Bishop North was looking at the ward list and learning who was in his ward, he was surprised as he came across Erica's name.

"Hey, Erica," Stuart said while cleaning out a mammoth mixing bowl in the bakery. "You know that I'm LDS, don't you?"

"Yeah," she said, not looking up from her work. Talk of religion was usually Erica's least favorite topic. Long ago she had decided against God. It wasn't that she necessarily thought there was no God, but if there was, she wanted nothing to do with Him.

"Well, Erica, they recently made me the bishop of the ward and as I was going over the ward list, I saw something that surprised me. I saw your name there."

"I'm not Mormon anymore," Erica said as she continued to work. "I went to primary when I was a kid, but that's about it. My parents got divorced. Life fell apart. That's about the whole story."

"We've talked a lot about life and struggles. Why didn't you ever tell me you were LDS?" he asked.

"Why? Would it have changed anything?"

"Of course not." He smiled. "Unless it would make you work harder."

"I doubt it would," Erica said. "Besides, I'm not really Mormon. You know about my past. You know how I feel about God. So what? Are you going to fire me now?" she asked, lightening the mood.

"I think it's illegal to fire someone because of religion," Stuart said back with a smile. "Besides I'm not sure I could find someone else to do your job the way you do it."

"That's true," Erica said, joining Stuart in his smile. "Slaves are hard to replace."

"But seriously, Erica," he said with his caring, sober side, which was never far off. "I think it would be great if you would come back to Church. You would find God filling the empty places in your life. You would find the healing you need."

Even after the years of deep respect and appreciation toward her employer, it took all Erica had in her not to get angry. She felt like saying, "*God doesn't have anything I need!*"

"Actually," Bishop North said after some time of awkward silence, "there might be something one step better than coming back to Church just yet. A handful of ward members are coming to my office this Sunday night."

"A punch and cookies gathering?" Erica joked.

"I'll even arrange for the punch and cookies if that will get you there."

"I'll think about it," Erica said lightly.

"I really hope you do," Bishop North said in his caring and sober manner.

"Deborah," Ken Richards said to his wife, "Bishop North wants us to come to his office at seven, Sunday night." Deborah slowly turned her gaze from the TV to an empty wall but made no indication that she had even heard. The year since they had found their son face down in the pool had been gut wrenching. Jimmy had been in the water for several minutes. The doctors were able to save his life, but his brain had died in many areas from the lack of air. For the first six months, the Richards had great hopes and faith that their son would be able to walk and talk again. The doctors recommended that they not medicate him much to relieve pain so they could see the extent to which Jimmy could be rehabilitated. But after months of various efforts, the doctors knew that very little would change in the future for the Richards' little boy. Making it all the more difficult, Jimmy's temperament changed, and he often cried out in mindless pain and frustration. Various medications made Jimmy easier to get along with, but those drugs did not help the parents much. Their mind-set of faith and hope soon dropped to feelings of immense despair and depression.

But there was another undercurrent in their relationship. Ken felt deep resentment toward his wife. He blamed her for not having a more watchful eye on their son that evening of the accident. Ken blamed her for the accident and for Jimmy's condition but would not dare express his bitterness. Though her husband said nothing, Deborah could feel his thoughts completely. It was the same loathing she had for herself.

When the accident first happened, they often held each other for support. But as the diagnosis became worse over the months, they grew apart. Deborah would notice that as she went to hold him, it was cold and without feeling. Then quickly he would find something he needed to do. Soon they both avoided any touch from each other.

"What does the bishop want?" Deborah finally asked after a long silence.

"I'm not sure," Ken replied stoically. "He talked about how he's been praying for us a lot and we've been on his mind. He wants us to come to his office Sunday night at seven o'clock. There will be some others there too. He made it sound like it's extremely important. Something we need."

"I've got to stay with Jimmy," Deborah said without emotion.

"I think I'm going to go," Ken said after some time. "Jimmy will be okay with the girls. I want you to come too. We need something to change."

"If it wasn't for what it would do to the kids . . ." Deborah paused and then decided not to finish her thought.

"Bishop called," Anna said to her husband, Mitch, who was sitting, watching a basketball game. "He wants us to come in to talk with him Sunday night at seven."

"Sorry, I'm not ready to be the Gospel Doctrine teacher," Mitch joked without breaking a smile.

"I doubt that's it." Anna smiled weakly. "He said he's been worried about us. I told him we would be there."

"What? Are you stupid?" Mitch shot out in anger. "Why are you such an idiot all the time? I'm not going. Go see your boyfriend by yourself!"

There was a time when Anna was hurt anew each time Mitch called her a name. But now, time had simply allowed her to apply a small layer of resentment to the old wounds surrounding her heart. *Is there really value in staying together for your daughter when all she will see is a loveless, cruel marriage like this?* Anna thought.

chapter six

THE GATHERING

"Thank you so much for coming tonight," Bishop North said as he looked at Ken Richards, Anna Johnson, and Erica Toplin. By looking at Bishop North, you could see a burden he bore. He wanted tonight to go the right way so badly. Bishop North had been fasting all day and pleading for the Lord's help to express the message he felt the Lord wanted him to share with this small group.

"It means so much to me that each of you came. There were a couple of others invited, but it seems that not all were able to make it." As Bishop North looked at the group, they could feel that quiet love that each had come to know from him. Bishop North's long, narrow office was lined with chairs that were used for various ward meetings. On one of the walls was a large white board. Instead of sitting at his desk, the bishop pulled a chair to sit in front of his desk. This made the group into more of a circle.

"I want each of you to know that you have been in my prayers more than you would imagine. Before I was called as bishop, I had little idea of the struggles and pain that so many in the ward were going through. As I prayed and pondered what the Lord would want me to do, I got an impression to call each of you together to talk about some things. Is it okay if we do that now?"

Anna and Ken nodded their heads. Knowing the Bishop's love and concern for them seemed to give him equity with the group that he could now spend. Those in the group knew Erica the least, due to the fact that she had not been to church since she was a child. Together the small group prayed.

"We all have different struggles," Bishop North said after the prayer. "But years ago someone taught me something that changed my life. I believe that it just might be the same lesson that will also bless your lives. I feel that the Lord wants me to share this message with you tonight. I thought about how to share the ideas and, as usual, the scriptures seem to do the best job."

"So what's the great lesson we need?" Brother Richards asked in a voice that seemed somewhat hard.

Bishop North smiled back at Brother Richards. "Strangely enough, the secret or lesson, has a lot to do with Anna's name."

"My name?" Anna wondered out loud.

"Do you know what your name means?" Bishop asked Anna.

"If I ever knew, I must have forgotten," Anna said timidly. Each person in the room had known the bishop long enough that they could talk comfortably, but still each felt some apprehension in meeting with the bishop tonight as a group.

"Your name holds a lesson that has the power to heal hearts, families, and each of our lives," Bishop North said with an earnest look in his eyes as he gazed at each one of them and then back at Anna. "Hidden in your name is something that changes everything it touches. It's the same thing that changed my life. This thing is something that changes every life that embraces it. It changes everything."

"Okay, Bishop," Anna said with a smile. "I'll take the bait. Tell us what this thing is that changes everything."

"I won't tell you," Bishop North said as he picked up a stack of library copies of the scriptures on his desk and passed them out. "I'll show you. Let's look at something together. I'm always impressed how the lessons for the people in the scriptures are the same lessons we need for the Lord to heal us. Now before we go anywhere in particular, I want you to think about the Israelites that Moses brought out of Egypt. As I'm sure you remember in the story, the Israelites were slaves in Egypt, where they suffered every kind of injustice. Egypt was a very wicked, worldly place. Now when God had Moses bring the Israelites out of Egypt, the Lord wanted to give them the fulness of the gospel." Bishop North stood and motioned to Erica. "Stand next to me for a second to help me illustrate."

Erica was taken off guard and gave a look of "Are you serious?" to Bishop North.

"Please, Erica," he encouraged. Reluctantly, she stood by the bishop and his desk. "Do you think you could step up onto my desk without using your hands or any helps?" Erica was shorter than most girls, being just over five feet tall. "Give it a try," Bishop said.

"You really want me to get on your desk?" Erica asked, feeling more than a little uncomfortable.

"In a single step without using your hands," Bishop clarified.

"This isn't what I expected when I decided to come," Erica said as she studied the table.

"Humor me," Bishop said with a small laugh. Erica stood closer to the desk and then, with a bit of a stretch, put one foot on the desk. Then with a last look at the bishop and the others watching her, she lunged up with her arms and tried to center her weight over her foot on the desk. It looked like she would make it till she started to tip and fell back to her other foot on the floor.

"What a disappointment," Ken said jokingly.

"That's okay, Erica," Bishop North said. "I don't think Brother Richards could do it either. But here's the point," Bishop North said as he went to the whiteboard and Erica sat back down. There he drew a picture.

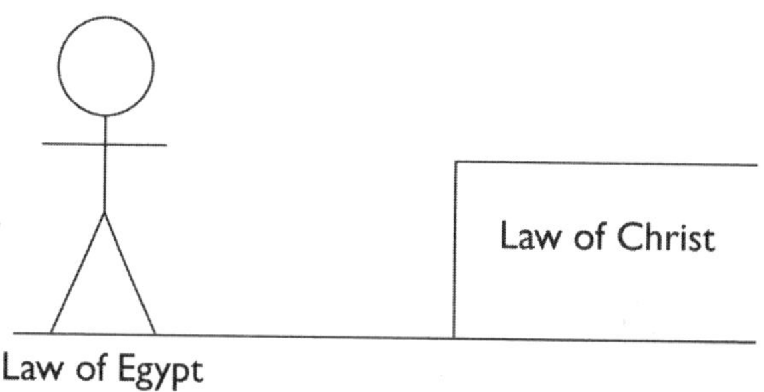

"It was also too big of a step for the Israelites. The Israelites were living in the wicked ways of Egypt. The Lord wanted to give them the fulness of the gospel right after they came out of Egypt. But the problem was that they couldn't go immediately from wickedness to Christlike living. So what did the Lord do? What step did the Lord give them to get them ready to eventually step further up and live the fulness of the gospel?"

"Law of Moses," Ken responded.

"Exactly," Bishop North said. He moved an empty chair up to the desk like it was a step up to his desk. He then also went to the whiteboard and added the step and its label.

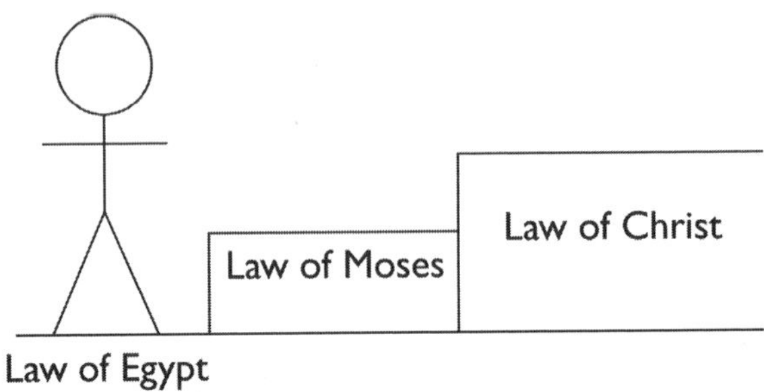

"Are the law of Moses and the Ten Commandments good things?" Bishop asked.

"Actually," Ken answered as he remembered what he had learned in law school, "most of the laws of our society have their start in the law of Moses."

"Right," Bishop confirmed. "Now let's turn from the Old Testament to the New Testament. Matthew chapter 5 is where Jesus teaches about the role the law of Moses plays for us. Egypt was a wicked place where murder, adultery, and injustice were very common. But what did the law of Moses say about those things, Brother Richards?"

"Thou shalt not kill, commit adultery, steal, etc."

"All wonderful laws," Bishop North added. "But here in the New Testament, Jesus starts to take the people to the next step. Instead of just refraining from killing, Jesus says to not even get angry. Instead of just avoiding adultery, Jesus takes it up a notch by teaching them to not even look upon another person in lust."

"This is great, Bishop," Ken Richards said. "But where's the point for us?"

"Right here is where it begins," Bishop North said with a faint glow, as if holding back excitement. "Look at verse 38 in chapter 5 of Matthew."

> Ye have heard that it hath been said, An eye for an eye, and a tooth for a tooth:

"Not only were things wicked in Egypt but also terribly unjust," Bishop North said. "Especially living as a slave. They had no rights and no one that could help. No justice. Moses had essentially said that the Israelites could have the justice of an eye for an eye and a tooth for a tooth. Punishments that would fit the crime. That is essentially how things are run in our society today."

"But today," Anna started to object, "if someone accidentally poked my eye out, I couldn't go poke out their eye."

"True," Brother Richards interjected with a laugh before the bishop could answer. "But you could sue for damages. If a doctor makes a mistake, or a product hurts us, we have the right to sue and get compensation to an equitable amount of money. If someone commits a crime, they'll have to pay their time in prison. In other words, justice. We have the right to get them back to the degree they hurt us."

"Well, when you put it that way, isn't that a good thing?" Anna asked. "That's justice. Getting what's right."

"Justice is good," Bishop North agreed, "but strangely, still not the best. Not the fulness of the gospel Jesus came to give."

"What do you mean?" Anna asked, shifting uncomfortably in her chair.

"Look for the justice in what Jesus goes on to say in the next verses."

> But I say unto you, That ye resist not evil: but whosoever shall smite thee on thy right cheek, turn to him the other also.
>
> And if any man will sue thee at the law, and take away thy coat, let him have thy cloke also.
>
> And whosoever shall compel thee to go a mile, go with him twain.
>
> Give to him that asketh thee, and from him that would borrow of thee turn not thou away.

"Where's the justice in those things?" Anna questioned with some sound of exasperation in her voice. Although her marriage had never been mentioned yet, it was in the forefront of her mind, knowing it was the reason she had been called there. "So if someone hits me, I shouldn't do anything back? If someone wants to take something from me, I should just let them?"

Bishop North looked into everyone's eyes, trying to see how they were all sorting out everything in their minds. "As difficult as it is, Jesus meant what He is saying to us here. If someone is going to take your coat, you should give him your sweater also."

Bishop added a question to the group, "Do you understand what the whole 'compelled to go a mile' part is about? In Jesus's day, the Jewish nation was occupied by the Romans. In Roman law, if a Roman citizen was traveling and carrying something, he could stop any Jew and make him or her carry his burden one mile and the Jew would have to oblige. Try to imagine doing what Jesus is saying here. After demanding your service and going a mile, the Roman says to you, 'Okay. You've done your part. I'll take it from here.' And then you say, 'It's okay, I'm headed in the same direction anyway. Let me carry this for you the rest of the way.' Imagine the shock on the Roman's face from your graciousness."

"I don't know if I could do that," Anna said, furrowing her brow. "If I were a Jew, I'm sure I would hate the Romans."

"And the Jews would have good reasons for hating the Romans. That is what makes what Jesus taught so revolutionary. It's funny," Bishop North continued, "the teachings of Jesus came and turned the world upside down and backwards."

Bishop North paused and looked over the small group of members he had called together. "Will each of you do something for me? I want you to think of a person who has hurt you more than anyone else. I won't be asking you to share who it is," Bishop added. "But nod your head when you have thought of the person you might have the hardest feelings toward." One by one, each of the three nodded, Erica being the last. "Now I want each of you to think of that person and what the Lord is telling you he wants you to do with that person as I read these next two verses.

> Ye have heard that it hath been said, Thou shalt love thy neighbour, and hate thine enemy.
>
> But I say unto you, Love your enemies, bless them that curse you, do good to them that hate you, and pray for them which despitefully use you, and persecute you;

After reading, Bishop North let silence punctuate the message for a few moments. "I wonder if there was ever a more challenging, difficult verse to live in all of scripture. Imagine those people who you have had hard feelings toward; now can you imagine loving them? Doing acts of kindness for them? Praying for them and wanting the best for them, despite how they have treated you?"

"Wait," Anna said quietly while the group was in thought. "I don't get it."

"What's that, Anna?" Bishop North asked, encouraging with a nod.

"You said that the law of Egypt was injustice and the law of Moses was justice. Then what is the law of Christ? What is higher than justice?"

Bishop North turned to the board and wrote in what she said, with a question mark under *Law of Christ.*

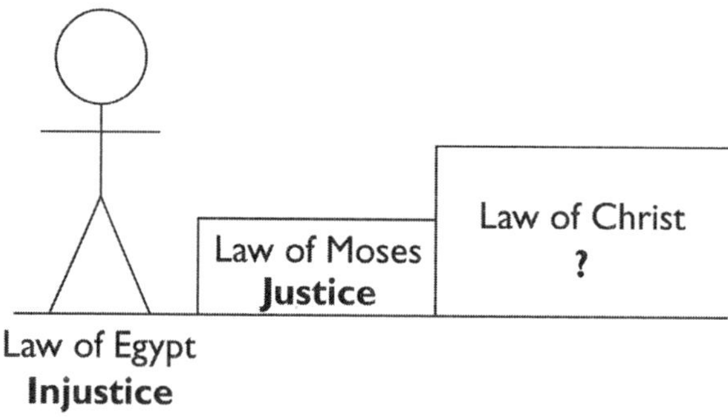

"That's it," Bishop North said as he looked at the group. "What Jesus is teaching in these verses is the grand secret. The solution. It's the thing that heals every heart that allows it in. It's what your name means, Anna," Bishop North said with a pause. "The name Anna means *grace.*"

"Wonderful," Anna commented quickly. "Grace. It figures that my name means a strange theological term that is hard to understand."

"Grace?" Brother Richards said with a questioning air in his voice. "I thought for sure you were going to say mercy was that last step."

"Grace isn't a term we use as much as mercy, but it has the elements of mercy," Bishop North replied. "But there is something more to grace. Mercy is to refrain from a negative consequence to another. If verse 44 was just referring to mercy, the Lord might have said:

> But I say unto you, *pay no attention to* your enemies, *don't curse back at* them that curse you, *ignore* them that hate you, and *think no*

> *evil to* those which despitefully use you and persecute you;

"But Jesus is asking us to go one step beyond mercy. He wants us to not only refrain from giving them back what they deserve, but He also wants us to be good to them."

"Then what does grace mean?" Erica asked, bursting somewhat into the conversation. The question came as a surprise since most of the discussion had been dominated by Ken and Anna. Bishop North smiled, pleased that Erica had joined in. Then he went to the board and turned to the group. "There are many definitions out there, and Webster has a few, but here is one that has worked well with the way history and the scriptures speak of grace." Then Bishop North wrote on the board:

> Grace: To be good to another without regard for what they have earned or merited, but rather according to what is in the best interest of the other person.

"In other words, it is just to be good to others."

"Isn't that just kindness?" Brother Richards asked in a condescending, corrective tone.

"Yes," Bishop North said with a smile. "Grace is a word that encompasses many other words. Grace is seen in words like *kindness*, *mercy*, *forgiveness*, *love*, and *generosity*. The additional element that grace includes is to give those things beyond what would be expected or deserved. Like Jesus is saying to do with our enemies."

"Doesn't grace have to do with salvation and things like that?" Brother Richards asked with a frown and a furrowed brow.

"Salvation is all about grace. We need to talk about that. But what I'm trying to express here is that grace isn't just about salvation. Grace is also about how God loves us every day and how He expects us to treat others. All of our lives we have been taught that we should try to be like our Heavenly Father and Jesus, right?"

"Of course," Brother Richards replied.

"Well, God isn't asking us to show a goodness or grace to others beyond how He treats us. In the next verse He says why we should treat others this way."

> That ye may be the children of your Father which is in heaven: for he maketh his sun to rise on the evil and on the good, and sendeth rain on the just and on the unjust.

"You see, God doesn't just send the blessing of rain and sunshine on those who do everything right. God is good to everyone and long suffering with us all. God shows kindness and mercy to good and bad people. That is how our Savior Jesus Christ has always loved us, despite our failings and mistakes.[1] Not because we are so good and wonderful all of the time, but because God is so good to us."

"I've got to admit," Brother Richards said with a sigh, "the term *grace* is still throwing me off. Although I can't say I've been able to come up with a working definition of grace in my mind, I'm not so sure of your definition."

"I understand," Bishop North said. "Perhaps grace is something we have often made too complex. Think back to a Shakespearean play. The way subjects would refer to kings and queens long ago is a perfect example. They would always use the title 'Your Grace.' The reason they used the title 'Your Grace' is that you could conclude that all the king did was out of grace. In theory, when a member of the kingdom would go to the sovereign king for help, he knew the king wouldn't help because he had to. If the king helped, it would be out of the goodness of his heart—the graciousness of the king.

"Consider another example. What does it mean when we say someone was a 'gracious host'?" Bishop North asked as he made quotation marks in the air with his fingers. "A gracious host receives that title when he or she has gone beyond what was expected. Likewise, if a popular girl went out with and was kind to a guy who wasn't as popular, we would say she 'graciously' accepted the date."

"This teaching of God, wanting us to be better to others than they might deserve, is the key; this teaching of grace is found everywhere in the scriptures. For instance, Christ's teaching of the Golden Rule is not 'Do unto others the way they have done unto you'—in other words, justice," Bishop added. "The Golden Rule is to treat others the way you would want others to treat you."[2]

"The term *grace* is just a little foreign to me," Brother Richards said.

"I agree," Anna said.

"That's okay," Bishop North replied. "What is important is understanding how God wants us to treat others, whether we call it grace or some other term. God wants us to show this goodness to others without regard for how they have treated us. God wants us to be good to others the way He has been good to us. Consider another verse," Bishop North said as he flipped through his scriptures. "In 1 Peter 3, verse 9 it says:

> Not rendering evil for evil, or railing for railing: but contrariwise blessing; knowing that ye are thereunto called, that ye should inherit a blessing.

"If injustice is returning *evil* for *good*, and justice is returning *good* for *good* and *evil* for *evil*, then grace is returning *good* for *evil*, and that is what the Lord is asking of us. That is what will change everything."

"Joseph Smith was a perfect example of this. Once there was a man named Elliott who was brought to the court in Nauvoo under the charge of having helped in kidnapping two Church members and swearing to kill Joseph. When the prophet saw Elliott's fear and helplessness, he had the charges dropped. After Joseph paid the man's fines, he brought the man to his own home, where he fed him and gave him a place to sleep. Joseph gave the man far better than he deserved. He showed this magnanimous kindness to other enemies as well."[3]

"So then," Bishop North began as he sat back in his chair, "what's the lesson for us? Everyone here has someone that they need to show grace to in order to find the healing he or she needs," Bishop North said. "Grace will change everything. God has someone you need to show goodness to."

Anna thought about her marriage. She had a hard time imagining throwing huge amounts of kindness toward her husband, who was verbally so hard on her. She thought that when getting married, Mitch would make her happy, but instead she felt that he had brought misery. *Now am I supposed to treat him like some great guy*? she fumed inside with her jaw clenched.

Ken thought about his resentment toward his wife for, as he saw it, neglecting their son and the resulting accident. *You can't just let things like that go,* he thought.

Erica thought about how she was abused and the hate she now had for that man in prison. But more than that, she held the greatest contempt for God who, in her eyes, let it happen in the first place. But now wasn't the time to throw out all of her objections. Not with these two strangers also here.

"So here is the invitation," Bishop North said in a clear voice. "I want to challenge each of you to extend grace and goodness toward that individual you have hard feelings toward. This is the direction the Lord is calling you to. This is the area wherein God is asking that your old self die and for you to become a new person. He's giving you a way to live as that new person as you interact with everyone around you.

"It's not like we're bad people, but this is impractical," Ken now said with clear anger in his voice. "This just doesn't work in our society. People can't live the way you're asking here."

"You're right," Bishop North said after a long pause and leaning forward. "Grace just doesn't make sense to the world. But Jesus means what He is asking us to do in these verses. Email me and let's talk. I want to know if you're willing to take this challenge. Let me know. But one thing I want you to know: this grace and goodness is what changes everything. It softens the heart and bends the knee. It changes everything.

"Go home and think about it," Bishop North said again as he stood up. "I'll get with each of you this week. I want to know how you feel about what we have talked about and if you are willing to take this challenge in a serious way."

Brother Richards stood and walked to the door. Before leaving he looked at Bishop North. "I really don't know if I agree with everything, but you do have me thinking. Still, I also have some things I have a problem with that I'll need to first resolve in my mind."

"I can't hope to win an argument with you, but let's definitely talk," Bishop North said with a serious smile as Ken walked out.

"See you tomorrow," Erica said as she walked toward the door. "But I'm not so sure you understand everything about my situation yet. And I'm not sure I want to tell you."

"When you're ready," Bishop said as he walked down the hall with her a few steps.

"Good night, Bishop," Anna said as she also left the office.

"So what do you think?" Bishop asked as he shook Anna's hand.

Anna smiled and then let go of his hand, turning to walk down the hall as if she didn't hear his question.

"Anna?" Bishop North asked, making sure she was all right. Anna stopped in the hall and then put her back against the wall.

Anna's red hair fell over her face, which she pulled back behind her ear.

"I don't think it will work, Bishop," Anna said, now looking up. The bishop could see a tear running down her face. "Not for Mitch and me. Not anymore."

NOTES

1. See also Luke 6:35 "But love ye your enemies, and do good, and lend, hoping for nothing again; and your reward shall be great, and ye shall be the children of the Highest: for he is kind unto the unthankful and to the evil." The part about "hoping for nothing again" is important in that acts of grace are not to manipulate someone to change.
2. For the Golden Rule, see Matthew 7:12 and Luke 6:31.
3. The following are a few examples of Joseph's gracious nature: "Elliot of Carthage . . . was arrested and brought before a court at Nauvoo. . . . This same Elliot had sworn to have the Prophet's life. . . . When the Prophet saw the man's fear and helplessness, he obtained a withdrawal of the charge, paid the costs himself, and invited Elliot to his own home to be fed and lodged" (George Q. Cannon, *Life of Joseph Smith*, 2nd edition [Salt Lake City: Deseret News, 1907], 456). Speaking at another time, Joseph explained about his enemies, "I have brought these men to Nauvoo, and . . . I have treated them kindly. I have had the privilege of rewarding them good for evil. They took me unlawfully, treated me rigorously, strove to deprive me of my rights, and would have run me into Missouri to have been murdered, if Providence had not interposed. But now they are in my hands; and I have taken them into my house, set them at the head of my table, and placed before them the best which my house afforded; and they were waited upon by my wife, whom they deprived of seeing me when I was taken" (Joseph Smith in *History of The Church of Jesus Christ of Latter-day Saints*, ed. B. H. Roberts [Salt Lake City: Deseret News, 1909], 5:467). When the Prophet was arrested by Reynolds and Wilson, he was brutally accosted. However, on their arrival in Nauvoo, Joseph Smith kindly treated them to a sumptuous meal in his own home. (See *History of the Church*, 5:460.)

chapter seven

A DIFFERENT KIND OF LOVE

"Would you like to talk some more, Anna?" Bishop North asked. Anna shrugged her shoulders. Bishop North went to the clerk's open office door. "Hey Jeff, can you stay just a bit longer?"

"No problem," the ward clerk said as he turned from his computer screen to face the bishop. Bishop North always made sure that he had someone next door in the clerk's office when talking with a woman or a youth in his office.

"Thanks, Jeff," Bishop North said. "It won't be long." Anna went back into the bishop's office and sat down.

"I'm sorry, Bishop, I'm sure you want to get back to your family."

"It's okay," he replied in a kind voice. "Eden knew I would be a little longer tonight."

"Your wife is one of the neatest people in the world," Anna said with conviction. "I hope you understand how lucky you are to have married such a great person. We're not all that lucky."

"She is wonderful," Bishop North replied. "But I am also sure that things can be wonderful again with you and Mitch."

"It's that easy to see Mitch and I have problems, isn't it?" Anna asked.

"Anna, you said you thought things wouldn't work. Do you mean about showing grace?" Bishop North asked. "Showing kindness and goodness toward him beyond how he treats you?"

"That's partly it," Anna said. "It's obvious why you invited

Mitch and me here tonight. I guess you have been able to see that our marriage isn't that great. I told Mitch you wanted to see us together, but he wouldn't come." Anna paused, considering how to say all the things that were on her mind. "Bishop, things haven't been good at all with us for a long time, but the thing that has been really ripping me apart about our marriage, in the last few days, has to do with a class I had at the college last week." Anna looked up to see the bishop smile and nod for her to continue.

"It's a family studies class that I'm taking for a credit I need for my degree in accounting." Anna began to feel a bit more comfortable talking about academics rather than herself. "A lot of the stuff in the class and the book have been really interesting. But last week the professor started to talk about the science of love. Can you believe that, people would actually study love like you would study atoms or economics?"

"Who knew?" Bishop North said with interest.

"Anyway, I guess people have actually done research and come up with theories of why people fall in love. Most of the theories about love really disturbed me. But maybe what disturbed me most is maybe they're right!"

"What did these theories propose?" Bishop North asked.

"One said that the way people meet and fall in love was like economics," Anna continued. "Where everyone comes with their goods—abilities, looks, traits, characteristics—and tries to strike the best deal in a relationship of what they can get, according to what they have to offer. If a person has many positive characteristics, they most likely will hold out for a relationship with someone who likewise has a lot to offer. He called it the 'Marriage Market.' "

"Interesting," Bishop North said. "So what do you think of these ideas?"

"I hated them," Anna said, "I've always enjoyed thinking that love was something mystical that no one could explain. But I also had to admit it seemed to explain a lot. Thinking back to my single years, it seemed true that people would try to get the best deal for themselves when looking to get married."

"A good investment. A high yield, low maintenance marriage," Bishop North inserted with a bit of a laugh.

"Exactly," Anna replied, with some surprise at how actively Bishop North was listening. "I guess so."

"But what has upset you so much?" Bishop asked.

Anna's enthusiasm with the conversation suddenly seemed to wane. "I don't know, Bishop. The past couple of days I've been thinking that maybe," Anna paused again. "Maybe I could have gotten a better deal for myself. Maybe I could have done better than marrying Mitch. There were so many things I didn't know about him when we got married so quickly. I couldn't see back then how we would be together—how miserable we would be together," Anna clarified. "We're so different."

Instead of responding immediately, Bishop North just looked into Anna's eyes. Anna quickly put her head down.

"I know I shouldn't feel that way. I'm ashamed with how I feel, but it doesn't seem to change it. It isn't something that just came up yesterday. For the past couple of years, our marriage has slowly been falling apart. I think we're both miserable. I don't want to live like this anymore, Bishop.

"I don't want to live like this," Anna repeated in a softer voice, realizing what she was saying. "So that's why I wanted to talk more with you." With the words sinking in of what she was saying, Anna began to cry with an occasional shudder in her shoulders. Bishop North didn't say anything but began to pray for Anna, seeking guidance from the Lord for what to do or say.

"It's kind of funny," Bishop said, "that your *family* studies class isn't doing a whole lot to keep your *family* together." Anna laughed in the middle of her sobbing with her head now on her hands. "It's pretty easy to see, Anna, that there is a big part of you that doesn't want to get a divorce."

"Because it's not just Mitch and I that it would affect," Anna said as another tear ran down her cheek. "I've thought about it so much. We have a child and families that we come from. It would have a terrible affect on so many more that just Mitch and me."

"So if I understand you right, you don't want a divorce," Bishop North clarified. "But are you really here because you want to fix your marriage?"

"I don't know. I'm so confused, Bishop," Anna said. "In a way, I wonder if fixing it is even a possibility."

"There is a big difference between someone who knows their marriage has problems and someone determined to try to fix it." Bishop North stated.

"I'm not sure I'm that second type. I'm not sure it can be fixed." Anna thought about how badly she had wanted to fix it through the last three years. It seemed impossible to remember when their marriage was really good, though she was sure there must have been those times. Yet it seemed even more difficult to imagine a good marriage in the future.

"God is really good at performing miracles," Bishop North said. "But I'm sure He is going to want your full commitment in changing your marriage first."

"I do want it," Anna said after some thought. "But it isn't just me in this marriage."

"God knows that. But your absolute commitment is essential."

"I'm afraid, though," Anna started. "Mitch and I aren't exactly new at this. Our marriage has been going in this bad direction for a long time."

"I'm sure it won't be easy," Bishop North said. "I'm sure there will be times ahead when God will challenge you on how badly you want it fixed. You reminded me of a wise old saying. 'No matter how long you've gone down the wrong road, turn back.' "[1]

Anna laughed at the simplicity of the logic but then frowned. "Maybe there is one alternative to turning back: bailing out."

"Divorce?" Bishop North clarified. "Satan tries to make divorce look like such an easy way to fix things. In the end though, people find it often creates bigger problems than they could possibly imagine—for themselves and everyone around them. Often people get a divorce hoping to start fresh in a new relationship. But they soon find that because they couldn't fix the problems in the past relationship, the same problems come back again.

"You know, your professor's theory does explain some things," Bishop continued. "But it especially explains why people would get a divorce."

"What do you mean?" Anna asked.

"If they felt they were no longer getting a good deal," he went on. "They would just look for a better deal and invest themselves with someone else. I see examples of that evil way of thinking about marriage increasing in our society."

"There isn't anyone else," Anna said, now looking sternly into the bishop's eyes to be sure he understood that. "There isn't anyone else. But I do see how other couples are and how kind and considerate they are to each other. And Mitch and I have moved so far from that, Bishop. It's gotten bad between us."

"It isn't like you hate each other, is it?" Bishop asked.

"Is apathy worse than hate?" Anna asked, not needing a response. "The resentment has been turning to hate, and maybe now it's turning to indifference. I'm beginning not to care at all about him," Anna added.

Bishop North paused in prayer, trying to think of what the Lord would have him say. Over time, he had learned to pull in the scriptures when counseling with an individual. From his brief experience as a bishop, and the many years with the Young Men, he had realized that when he used the scriptures, a point would sink in more deeply and powerfully than just verbally reasoning out the same point with a person. A scripture turned on the lights of understanding more quickly for any person he was counseling with. After some thought, a scripture about marriage came to his mind. "Let me show you a powerful scripture about marriage," Bishop North said as he opened the scriptures on his desk.

"It's Ephesians 5, verse 25," he said, moving through the pages. "This is the Apostle Paul speaking to husbands, but the advice goes both ways. Anna, look for what this is saying to you about your marriage." The bishop handed the scriptures over for her to read herself.

> Husbands, love your wives, even as Christ also loved the church and gave himself for it.

"So what do you think?" Bishop asked.

"If the advice is the same for wives, then it seems it's saying I need to love more," Anna said, not feeling overly impressed with the verse as she handed the scriptures back to him.

"True," Bishop said, motioning for her to keep holding the scriptures. "But more than saying the degree we should love, it's describing *how* we are to love. Look at it again."

Anna looked back over the verse but this time the word "as" stood out to her. Love our spouses as Christ loves. "We are to love like Christ does," Anna stated. "But that's what I said. We should love a lot more."

"It's not just that the Lord loves more than we do," Bishop North said. "His love is fundamentally different from the way other people love. The nature of His love is different."

"What do you mean?" Anna asked, starting to feel her curiosity rise a bit.

"You shared with me that theory about how people love," Bishop said. "Is that how Christ also loves, except He loves more intensely?"

Anna thought about the theory about how people try to see what they can get out of a relationship. "No," she said. "I hope that's not how the Savior loves us."

"You're right," Bishop North said. "But thinking about how people often love might give us a chance here to discover how truly different God's love is. Your professor was trying to teach why people love and do things for each other. Let's look at why Jesus did what He did for us. What motivated the very Son of God to bend so low and undergo the agony and Atonement that He did? What inspired the Lord Jesus Christ to descend from His heavenly throne, suffer, and die for you and me? There is usually a motivation for what we do. What was His motivation?"[2]

Anna shrugged her shoulders after some thought.

"How about this?" the bishop continued with a smile. "I'll give a worldly view about love and we then can compare that to the Lord's love. So with that in mind, was the reason the Lord decided that He would suffer and die for us because we loved Him so much? Just imagine in the premortal life how we must have looked up to, admired, and loved our eldest brother, Jesus Christ. When the Father presented His plan and the need for a redeemer, Jesus stepped forward and said that He would sacrifice for all of us who adored Him so much. We find it easy to love those who love us. We find it is a great deal easier to sacrifice for those who love us. Surely Jesus would die for so many who loved Him. Do you think that was the reason, Anna?"

"You're asking if Jesus decided to die for us because we loved him so much?" Anna confirmed.

The Bishop nodded his head.

"I want to say no."

"You're right," the bishop said as he turned in his scriptures to another place. "In 1 John 4:19, the order of who loved whom first is stated. It says:

> We love him, because he first loved us.

"You see," the bishop continued, "our wonderful Savior, Jesus Christ, was already in love with us, long before we even knew to love Him in return. He was showing us His love and devotion long before we grew to love Him so much in the pre-earth life. It would be nice to be able to say that the Savior died for us because we love Him so much, but quite the opposite was true. He died on a cross mostly surrounded by those that had despised and rejected Him. The scriptures say of His life on earth that:

> He is despised and rejected of men; a man of sorrows, and acquainted with grief: and we hid as it were our faces from him; he was despised, and we esteemed him not.[3]

"Anna," the bishop said with a far-off look on his face. "I remember in a class I had in college learning something similar to what your professor said. They did a study where they set up a beautiful young woman by the side of the road with a broken-down car. Then they counted how many would stop to help. Then they took the same beautiful young woman and did things to make her less attractive, and then they saw how many would stop to help her. They found that people are more likely to help those that are perceived to be beautiful. Could it be that Jesus decided to suffer and die for us because we were so beautiful?"

"I don't think God sees beauty the same way we do," Anna said.

"I think you're right. A scripture I memorized in seminary, a long time ago, said,

> For the Lord seeth not as man seeth; for man looketh on the outward appearance, but the Lord looketh on the heart.[4]

"So, like you, I've wondered," the bishop continued, "if the Lord sees beauty differently than how we do, with our mortal eyes; then I wondered if beauty to Him is more a factor of a person's goodness and kindness. I also wonder if sin tarnishes one's appearance to the immortal eye. Think of how Jesus saw us as He was in Gethsemane and as He hung on the cross. He was not seeing us at our best, but at our worst. He was suffering for our sins. He was experiencing our lowest and most shameful moments in sin. He was coming to know us in all the wretchedness of our sins. That is how He saw us on the cross."

Bishop North paused a moment, looking at Anna, who was thinking about her failings in life. "Anna," he said, "I was told once that 'a friend is someone who knows you perfectly and loves you anyway.' Never has that been truer than with the Savior when He died for us, His friends. Not because we were so beautiful and attractive, and not because we loved Him, but because of our desperate need. All sinners, all guilty, all hopeless, and all completely lost without His grace."[5]

"I'm sorry," Bishop North said, looking at Anna in thought. "I'm sure I'm talking too much."

"No, you're not at all," Anna said. "It's just a lot to think about."

"Do you want one last idea of how God's love is different from how most people love?" he asked.

"Absolutely," Anna replied.

"You were saying that your professor's theory was that people will love those that they will get the most from in return. Could it be that the Lord suffered and died for us because He knew He would get back so much in return for His sacrifice? Perhaps He knew that we would one day praise and worship Him for what He did for us. Possibly Jesus understood we would build churches throughout the world and temples in His name. Maybe He knew of all the hymns and songs we would write of Him and all the prayers offered in thanks for Him. Perhaps the Savior discerned that people would decidedly become followers of Him forevermore and dedicate their entire lives to Him. Perhaps Jesus knew He would receive back so much in return for His sacrifice that it was worth it. Just like people often give and serve because of what they will receive in return. Could that be the reason He did all He did for us?"

"I hope not," Anna said.

"A scripture in the Book of Mormon clarifies this one," the bishop said as he started to turn to a different scripture. "Here in Mosiah 2:20–21 it says,

> I say unto you, my brethren, that if you should render all the thanks and praise which your whole soul has power to possess, to

> that God who has created you, and has kept and preserved you, and has caused that ye should rejoice, and has granted that ye should live in peace one with another—
>
> I say unto you that if ye should serve him who has created you from the beginning, and is preserving you from day to day, by lending you breath, that ye may live and move and do according to your own will, and even supporting you from one moment to another—I say, if ye should serve him with all your whole souls yet ye would be unprofitable servants.

"It is essentially saying, Anna, that if you and I were, from this moment on, to live perfectly, and devote every moment and breath in doing all we could for the Savior, we would still be 'unprofitable servants.' And think about what the word 'profit' means."

"Gross earnings, minus expenditures," she said with a smile. "My economics classes are a bit easier to understand."

"Then what does that say about us and the Savior?" he asked.

Anna thought for a moment, putting the idea of profit in a completely different context. "It means that what we can give back to the Lord will never equal what it personally cost Him to save us individually."

"Yes. It means that it took more of His blood and sweat, effort and tears, suffering and sorrow, to save us than we will ever be able to give Him back in return," the bishop added. "More effort was spent in order to save us than we can ever return to Him in praise, love, and devotion."[6]

"So, in a sense, does that mean we were bad investments to the Lord?" Anna asked.

The bishop laughed at the severe conclusion to the thought. "Would it make you feel bad to think of yourself that way?"

"I guess it could," Anna said after some thought. "But actually it kind of makes me feel good. It makes me feel loved. Really loved."

"So if Jesus could not have had any of those ulterior motives," Bishop asked, "why then did He suffer and die for you, Anna?"

Anna thought about it. "It's because He loves me with unselfish, pure love."

"So back to our scripture," Bishop North said. " 'Husbands, love your wives, even as Christ also loved the church and gave himself for it.' To love 'as Christ' loved is fundamentally different from the way the world loves. That's the grace we were talking about earlier. Grace is being good to a person, loving a person," Bishop North clarified, "not because that's what they deserve, or earned with you, but because you love them and you want what's best for them. That is the love and grace that God has shown us—impractical grace."

"What do you mean by 'impractical'?" Anna asked.

"This way of loving and being good to others just doesn't make sense to the world. Jesus came and showed the world a love that is baffling. For instance, Anna, you know I think you're great," Bishop North said with sincerity. "But consider if I were different to you. What if I didn't like you and whenever I met someone you knew, I would gossip and make up lies about you. Would you find it a bit more difficult to like me?"

"I guess I would," Anna replied.

"Well, what about the opposite?" he continued. "What if every time I saw you I asked how you were doing, complimented you, and told everyone, all the time, how wonderful you are? And by the way, Anna, I really do think you are wonderful," Bishop clarified. "Would you find it easier to like me back?"

"Sure, no problem," Anna responded.

"That is how people in the world generally love," the bishop went on. "Most people love those who love them and return hate to those who hate them. By the way, your professor wasn't the first to come up with those ideas of how people love. Jesus brought out the idea almost two thousand years earlier. Jesus expressed the idea when talking about publicans. They were the tax collectors in that society and were considered among the most wicked and immoral people. Jesus talked about them right after the verse we looked at earlier tonight in Matthew 5. He said:

> For if ye love them which love you, what reward have ye? do not even the publicans the same?
>
> And if ye salute your brethren only, what do ye more than others? Do not even the publicans so?

"In other words Jesus is saying, 'Anyone can love those who love them, and most people do. But I want you to love even those who don't love you. Be good to everyone, even if they don't deserve it.' That's grace. And it is what real love is all about."

"So you want me to love Mitch, not the way he deserves or loves me, but rather love him and be good to him despite everything?" Anna said in conclusion after some silence. "Love him unconditionally."

"It's not me, Anna," Bishop North clarified again. "It's what the Lord is saying to you here in the scriptures."

Anna leaned forward with her hands to her chin. "Unconditional love. My professor also mentioned his thoughts about unconditional love."

"Oh really?" Bishop North replied with a sound of sarcastic surprise.

"He asked the whole class to raise their hands if they believed in unconditional love. Most everyone did. Then he picked one of the older ladies in the class and asked her if she was married and if she had unconditional love for her husband. She said she was married but that she wasn't sure if her love was unconditional. So he then asked if there was anything he could do that would cause her to stop loving him. She replied that there probably was, so he said, 'Then it's not unconditional love. It is dependent on how he treats you.' "

"Then he asked her to name someone she had unconditional love for. She said she did for her son. Then the professor asked if there was anything he could do to cause her to stop loving him. 'Nothing,' she replied. Then he said, 'What if he went off and brutally and painfully killed every other member of your family? Would you still love him?' She said she thought she still would love him. Then he asked if she would even love him slightly less. After some thought she said she thought she might love him a little less. Then he quickly concluded again that her love was conditional, to some degree, on his behavior, so again her love wasn't truly unconditional. So was he right, Bishop? Is there really unconditional love? Could I really have that for Mitch or anyone else?"

Bishop North sat back and looked at a picture of the Savior on the sidewall of his office. "Sometimes I am not very comfortable with the term 'unconditional love' because some mistakenly take the idea to mean that God will bless without conditions.[7] This is not true, but for the sake of what happened, let's use that term. Maybe it wasn't *what* he was asking about unconditional love, but *who* he was asking," Bishop North said after some thought. "Your professor didn't ask the question to God, but rather, to one of us mere mortals. We aspire to love with unconditional love, but it is hard to always be there on that level. On the other hand, isn't it interesting how close that mother's love was to being unconditional? Your professor had to contrive a pretty far-fetched scenario before that mom flinched."

"Let me show you a scripture that reminds me of what you said," Bishop North said as he looked through his scriptures. "Here is one of those absolute gems we find in Isaiah. In Isaiah 49:14–15 the Israelites were feeling forgotten and forsaken by God, but the Lord says back to them:

> Can a woman forget her sucking child, that she should not have compassion of the son of her womb? yea, they may forget, yet will I not forget thee.

"Of all the things the Lord could compare His love to, He compares it to a mother's love. A few minutes ago we were saying that the Savior's love is different. We concluded that He didn't love us because we first loved Him. Likewise, He didn't love us because we were so pure and perfect all the time, nor because we give back so much in return. Isn't that how your love for your daughter, Caitlin, is?"

Anna thought about her three-year-old daughter. Images spun through Anna's mind as a faint smile crossed her face.

"Did you wait for her to love you before you decided that you would love her?" Bishop North asked.

Anna thought about when Caitlin was born. They asked Mitch to help cut the umbilical cord. Then they wrapped Caitlin in blankets and placed her on Anna's stomach and chest. Despite all the exhausting pain, Anna could still remember the tears that rolled down her cheeks and the love she felt. "No, I loved her immediately with all my heart. I would still do anything for my daughter. Even die for her."

"So you don't love her because she loved you first," Bishop concluded out loud. "Do you love her so much because she does everything right all the time?"

"No," Anna said. "She can be quite the handful, but I still love her more than anything."

"Is part of that love you have for her based on all you figure she will one day do for you in return?" Bishop asked. "Do you think the love you are putting into her will be well worth it because of all the love she will one day give back to you?"

Anna laughed as she shook her head. "I'm no expert on kids like I'm sure you and your wife are, but already, I'm pretty sure we will put more effort and love into her than we will ever get back in return."

"Then you see that you have a large measure of grace for your daughter. As her parent, you want what's best for her. You want her to succeed. You're positively disposed toward her. You want what's good for her and you want to take her side and help things work out for her. You naturally favor her as your daughter.

"And in that," Bishop North went on, "you're beginning to see the love and care God has for us. On our best days of being good parents, we only start to approach how good of a parent God is. If we, imperfect parents, love our children like you described, how much more incredible is our Heavenly Father's love for us? You are your Heavenly Father's daughter, Anna. At our very best, our love for our children can only start to approach the divine love God has for us.

"Now, Anna," Bishop North concluded, "God doesn't just want us to be impressed with the way He loves us. He wants us to go and do likewise. This is the way the Lord wants you to try to love Mitch. Like I said earlier, you go and love Mitch this way, and you'll see that it will start to change everything. Although what the Lord is asking you to do here is very difficult, I know you can do it. Pray for His strength and He will help you. Will you try to show Mitch this grace?"

NOTES

1. Turkish proverb.
2. It is important to understand Christ's motivations. We are taught, "We may never understand nor comprehend in mortality *how* He accomplished what He did, but we must not fail to understand *why* He did what He did" (Ezra Taft Benson, "Jesus Christ—Our Savior and Redeemer," *Ensign*, June 1990, 4).
3. Isaiah 53:3
4. See 1 Samuel 16:7.

5. See Psalm 14:3.
6. Concerning Christ's motives, Spencer W. Kimball stated: "Never did the Savior give in expectation. I know of no case in his life in which there was an exchange. He was always the giver, seldom the recipient. Never did he give shoes, hose, or a vehicle; never did he give perfume, a shirt, or a fur wrap. His gifts were of such a nature that the recipient could hardly exchange or return the value. His gifts were rare ones: eyes to the blind, ears to the deaf, and legs to the lame; cleanliness to the unclean, wholeness to the infirm, and breath to the lifeless. His gifts were opportunity to the downtrodden, freedom to the oppressed, light in the darkness, forgiveness to the repentant, hope to the despairing. His friends gave him shelter, food, and love. He gave them of himself, his love, his service, his life. The wise men brought him gold and frankincense. He gave them and all their fellow mortals resurrection, salvation, and eternal life. We should strive to give as he gave" (Edward L. Kimball, ed., *The Teachings of Spencer W. Kimball* [Salt Lake City: Deseret Book, 1982], 246–47).
7. Elder Russell M. Nelson articulated the danger of the term 'unconditional love' in an article, "Divine Love," *Ensign*, Feb. 2003, 20.

chapter eight

SAVING GRACE

In other words, Bishop wants me to be nicer to my wife, Ken stewed to himself as he looked out his law office window at the street and people below. *But he has no idea what it's like.* Ken's wife, Deborah, had changed after the accident. Ken felt it was bad enough that through her neglect, she had caused their son Jimmy to be permanently handicapped. But now Deborah had become neglectful and apathetic about every aspect of life. She did little to clean the house or care for their two girls. Everything fell to Ken, which he felt was more than he could handle at times. Lately he had even hired a maid to come in weekly and clean. There were days that he had come home and seen that she had not even gotten dressed from her pajamas. And now the bishop was saying he wasn't kind enough? *I do it all at home.*

There was a knock at the door. "Come in, Nancy," Ken said.

"How are you?" Ken's secretary asked as she smiled at him. She then walked over to a filing cabinet in the corner.

"Not terrible, I suppose," Ken said as he turned from the window to face Nancy. "And you?"

"You always have to push ahead," she replied.

"That's so true," Ken responded in almost a whisper. He was always impressed with how his secretary kept herself up and looked nice. Her life wasn't exactly easy but she worked hard and made the best of things.

"Well, I'm glad things are going well for you. You deserve it more than most anyone I know," Ken said, turning his gaze away from Nancy back to the street below.

Ken jolted in surprise as he felt Nancy's hands on his shoulders, rubbing them. "You deserve good things too. I hope things get better," Nancy said as she gave a last soft squeeze to his shoulders and then walked out, closing the door. Ken sat stunned as he slowly exhaled.

What was that? Ken thought in shock. *Maybe it was nothing.* Nancy had always been more affectionate toward people than most. After reflecting on the experience, Ken concluded that it was probably nothing in his secretary's mind. But despite what it might have meant to her, Ken couldn't help but admit to himself, that it was colossal to him. No one had touched him like that in his twenty years of marriage except his wife. And his wife hadn't even shown him warmth like that for many months. Ken had always kept the strictest standards of morality and boundaries with coworkers and clients. But he couldn't stop thinking of Nancy's gentle touch. At the moment, he couldn't recall receiving affection like that in so long. *I want that too,* he thought. *Don't I deserve someone also who—*

No! He stopped himself. *I have a family. What about my children? I'm not going to ruin my family more than it's been ruined.* Then Ken thought that over the last year, his marriage had been going toward ruin in many ways. Then he thought again about Nancy's touch and her squeeze on his shoulders.

For the last year Ken had gotten along and made do with the difficult situations, but now he saw he could no longer endure. Her touch, whether innocent or not, was like cold water, waking him up to his situation. Life could not remain as it had been or was now.

Ken stood up and started to pace. In his mind, he saw two paths for his life, and neither were the path he had been on. On the one path, he could see his marriage ending, keeping the kids, and reconstructing his life with someone else. This path seemed clear but awful. Although he felt he deserved better than how Deborah had become, there was pity for what this would do to her. What would become of Deborah?

Then on the other path, it seemed very vague and unclear. "Grace will change everything," Ken remembered Bishop North saying in his office. *I don't see how it could change anything,* he thought to himself.

"Take care of yourself, Mr. Richards," Nancy said as Ken left his office in the late afternoon. Strangely, Ken felt at a loss for words as he saw her and her caring smile again. "Thank you, Nancy," he said with a strange sincerity. Again he knew that life could not continue as it had been. Something had to give. Things had to change.

As Ken came home, he walked up the sturdy ramp that had been built over the front two steps to his house. The Richards' house had seen a few changes since Jimmy's mobility had become a wheelchair.

"Has Jimmy had his exercise?" Ken asked as he came in the room where his wife sat at the computer. But instead of looking at the screen, her head was down in her hands. Since the accident, Jimmy's physical therapist had given a variety of exercises they were to go through with Jimmy to keep his body strong and to attempt to reestablish reflexes as much as possible.

"Not his legs," Deborah replied after a few moments, as she lifted her head from her hands and stared up at the ceiling. "I'll finish with it in a few minutes."

As Ken looked at his wife, his mind went back to things the bishop said. Ken thought about saying thank you for what she had done, and all the other kind things a good husband should say and do. But something in him just couldn't. Resentment toward his wife had ruled his heart and the thought of changing seemed absurd.

"I see you're busy," he said in a condemning, sarcastic tone. "I'll finish it."

As Ken walked into the front room he saw his small, six-year-old son looking out the large window where the sun had set a few hours before.

"Hey, Jimmy," Ken said in a forced enthusiastic voice. "How goes it?" With a rocking motion, Jimmy slowly turned his head and smiled.

"Did you have a good day, buddy?" Ken asked, not expecting

any further response beyond the smile. "Well, I can't leave you in here. Let's go in my office," Ken said, releasing the wheel brake and starting to push Jimmy's chair. Originally, the Richards and the doctors had hoped that Jimmy would soon have enough motor control to be able to direct a motorized wheelchair, but over the last year that hope had vanished. "Sit here, buddy," Ken said as he stopped his son in his home office, which sometimes doubled as a guest bedroom, with a bed to one side. There Ken took off the Velcro straps that held his son straight in his chair and then laid him on the bed. This spare bed was often used by Ken also. As Ken pushed on Jimmy's feet, trying to get him to push back, he looked at collages of pictures on the office walls and thought of past times together. It wasn't always like this with Deborah. Life was happy before. But that was a long time ago. After Jimmy's therapy, Ken placed him back into his chair and put some toys on the tray of his wheelchair for him to scoot around.

As Ken sat down, he looked to the side of his immaculate home office to the dark oak shelves where he displayed items he had brought back from his mission in Scotland. The items on the shelves brought strong memories.

"He's wrong," Ken said out loud as he thought about the bishop's words and pondered things he had learned and taught on his mission. "He's got his doctrine all wrong. Grace: that's just not how the gospel works." Ken was just about to grab his scriptures on the shelf and look up the verses he was thinking of. Then he stopped and thought again of Nancy's hands on his shoulders. He pulled back his hand and felt a tug in his heart.

"I hope my order didn't throw your day off," Ken said as he walked into the bishop's bakery and sandwich shop. "I just thought last night that I should treat my staff to lunch today."

"Glad we could take your order this morning. But I hope our discussion Sunday night wasn't some subconscious form of advertising fresh sandwiches."

"If it was, would I get it all for free?" Ken joked. Bishop North only smiled.

"Tell me Ken, how is your wife, Deborah?" Bishop North's

question suddenly changed the mood. Ken tried to keep the smile he had on his face, but slowly the joy leaked out of it as he looked down at the empty counter in front of him.

"I don't think she has really had a good day since the accident," Ken said after some thought.

"Are you taking care of her, Ken?" Bishop North said with a concerned look, grabbing hold of Ken's aimless stare.

"Bishop, I have some concerns with what you were talking about the other night," Ken said with a desire to change the subject. "About grace and the gospel. I think there are some doctrinal problems with the points you made." Ken was surprised to see no sign of defensiveness in Bishop North's face.

"Care to sit in my office now to talk about it?" Bishop offered. Ken nodded in agreement.

"Erica, can you finish this order?" Bishop North called across the store.

"No problem, boss," Erica said in a careless tone as she looked back and recognized Ken from the other night.

"Sorry, this isn't the most comfortable office," Bishop North said as Ken stepped into a surprisingly small room, which barely seemed to fit a desk, a filing cabinet, and two chairs. "I don't spend much time in here."

"Don't worry, Bishop," Ken replied. "I wish I spent far less time in my office."

"Tell me what you're thinking about Ken," Bishop North said, getting to the point.

Ken swallowed and looked down, gathering his thoughts. "Sunday night, I don't think I agreed with many of the things you said. I was just going to blow it off as a doctrinal disagreement, but something has made it so I can't seem to leave it alone."

"What's happened?" Bishop North asked after a long pause.

"It's nothing really," Ken said with a meager smile, trying to lighten the mood in the room. "My secretary, Nancy, is just a naturally affectionate girl. She put her hands on my shoulders and started to rub them. After a few moments she stopped and went out. But I must admit, it got me thinking."

"You leave her alone, Ken!" Bishop North rebuked in a changed voice and appearance that froze Ken in his place. Bishop's North's eyes bore down on him in a fierce look, causing fear to completely overtake Ken so he couldn't speak or move. It wasn't a fear that Bishop North was going to strike him. It was a fear of absolute peril, not to the body but to something deep down inside. To Ken, it was as if an angel had rebuked him.

There Ken sat, chest heaving, yet he couldn't look away from the bishop's brutal stare. Finally Ken could only look away as he broke into tears and sobbed. "I know," he cried. "I know. I decided long ago never to entertain feelings like that. I didn't do anything, Bishop," Ken offered as an appeasement. "I don't want to do anything. But I have felt like I am at the crossroads of my life here. For the first time, I'm really wondering if Deborah and I can last. I don't know if I can keep going like this. And then at the office—"

"Ken," Bishop interrupted with a strong, but calmer voice. "We will talk about life and how things can get better between you and Deborah, but you have to promise me, Ken, that you are going to keep yourself away from that woman in every way. You have no idea of the misery and absolute chaos Satan wants to employ in your life here. Don't even let yourself think about her."

"Yes," Ken said slowly, knowing his bishop knew of the evil that had taken a hold in his heart.

"Now do you see the need for grace between you two?" Bishop North asked. "The grace to forgive—and Deborah is also going to need the grace to forgive you."

"I didn't *do* anything, Bishop," Ken defended, not sure if the bishop understood what he had just confessed.

"I'm not talking about what happened in your office," Bishop clarified. "Forgive you for how you have treated her over this last year."

Despite the penitent feelings he was feeling with the bishop, Ken felt defensive at his bishop's remark. "What do you mean?"

"Tell me about your resentment," Bishop replied instead of answering Ken's question.

As Ken already knew, his bishop could see a lot into his marriage and family.

"I've had a lot of bitterness," Ken admitted stoically.

"She's been through so much too. Have you been the support she's needed? Have you forgiven her and shown her your love?"

What about what I've needed? Ken thought to shoot back, but instead he sat there. "Okay, you're right. But I have some serious reservations with all that you were saying about grace. I know you're saying I need to show grace and kindness to her, but I don't buy everything you're saying about showing grace. I don't think you have it completely right. I don't think I can do what you are asking if I honestly don't agree with the doctrine of what you are saying."

"Certainly," Bishop said. "Then let's talk through those concerns."

When Ken first thought about discussing these concerns, they were more objections, and he imagined himself feeling more forceful. But now his feelings were somewhat tempered. "I have a problem with how you are talking about grace and God. I don't think God gives grace the way you are saying. Especially in the context of salvation."

"Ken," Bishop started as he wiped a bit of flour from his hand onto his white apron. "My point in talking about grace the other night was to clarify how God wanted us to treat those around us, not to get into a theological debate about grace and salvation."

"But you can't separate the two," Ken objected. "Correct doctrine is universal. If grace applies to our fellow man, then it also has to apply to our salvation in the same way. You were talking about how God manifests His grace to us, but what you were saying just isn't how it works with salvation."

"I'm not sure what you mean," Bishop North replied.

"I served a mission in Scotland," Ken said. "There I met a lot of people with strange ideas about grace and salvation. I also learned a lot about how God blesses us, and it isn't according to grace, the way you are suggesting."

"So how is it?" Bishop asked. "How do you think God blesses us?"

"Two scriptures I learned well," Ken said as he grabbed the bishop's scriptures on the desk and started to turn. Bishop North kept a pair of scriptures at the bakery in case he had some time to read during a break or in case a ward member came by. "Doctrine and Covenants 130:20–21." Ken read:

> There is a law, irrevocably decreed in heaven before the foun dations of this world, upon which all blessings are predicated—
>
> And when we obtain any blessing from God, it is by obedience

to that law upon which it is predicated.

"So when we get blessings from God, it is because of obedience to those particular commandments for those blessings. And the other verse completing the thought is Doctrine and Covenants 82:10."

> I, the Lord, am bound when ye do what I say; but when ye do not what I say, ye have no promise.

"So when we get blessings from God, it is because we were obedient in the right areas. I even remember," Ken went on with a small smile and a far-off look on his face, "that we would 'bind the Lord.' When my companion and I wanted more people to teach or to get a certain family baptized, we would 'bind the Lord' by being extra obedient, fasting, and praying. You know: all those missionary things. You said God gives to people according to what is good for them and in their best interest, regardless of what they deserve. But I learned that God gave us according to what we earned."

"Sounds like a pretty good plan," the bishop said with a smile he seemed to be trying to control. "But how well did it actually work—with the baptisms and people to teach? Were you able to get God to bless you the way you wanted?"

Ken gave a short laugh. "Missionary work can be difficult in Scotland. I'm sure it did work sometimes. But not as often as I would have hoped. I'm sure I wasn't the perfect missionary."

"That's an interesting idea to 'bind the Lord,' " Bishop North said, making quotation marks with his fingers. "When you say *bind*, I can't help but think of tying down or confining. Can we put a leash on God? Can we, as mortals, bind and control an all-powerful, sovereign God to control His granting of blessings?"

"Bishop," Ken said defensively, "I didn't come up with the idea. I was taught it, and it's in the scriptures."

"Let's look at those scriptures again in a minute," Bishop North said. "But consider what you are saying here. Excuse the frankness, but doesn't this doctrine reduce God down to being a genie in a bottle, where if we follow some guidelines, we can control Him to do our will? Instead of a sovereign God, He becomes our tool to manipulate in order to get what we want. But He isn't our great spiritual vending machine in the sky, where we put in our two quarters of good works and select what we want. We can't bind or yoke the Lord to control His giving of blessings."

Ken's mind raced. As a lawyer, he usually could say something in a disagreement. But part of him didn't want to. "I don't know if it really makes Him into a genie or vending machine," Ken defended.

"Perhaps not," Bishop said with a smile. "But it seems to me that God is the master of all heaven and earth, and we are to be his servants. We are to be the instruments in His hands and never the other way around! It is His wants that must be followed. It is His will that must be pursued. He is the parent, and we are the children. He is the Master and we are the servants. He is the Lord and we are the subjects—never the other way around. Worst of all, the idea of binding the Lord for blessings seems like us getting the Lord to do something He was not naturally inclined to do in the first place, as if He were on a different team or something."

"Okay, good points," Ken said, feeling a bit more defensive. "But it *is* in the scriptures. We can't just cut out the verses we disagree with or don't like."

"You're right," Bishop North said with a smile again. He noticed that when in a discussion, he had to often slow down and not let himself get contentious. He felt that if the Spirit could not be there for everyone, there would be no success, no matter how good the line of reasoning was. "Let's look at that first scripture again. There is something I found that I used to miss when reading the verse. It says:

> There is a law, irrevocably decreed in heaven before the foundations of this world, upon which all blessings are predicated—
>
> And when we obtain any blessing from God, it is by obedience to that law upon which it is predicated.

"I used to read the verses like you did, that there were many laws and commandments and that obedience to particular ones determines the bestowal of certain blessings. Many actions resulting in many different reactions. But notice at the beginning it says that there is 'a law.' The next verse makes it clear again that it is one law. And this one particular law, or principle, governs how the Lord grants blessings. So what is this single law that governs how

God grants blessings?"

"I'm not sure," Ken conceded, still trying to think of the verse differently.

"Consider for a moment that the law by which He gives us blessings is simply that God gives what is in our best interest, based on what we have shown by our obedience."

"Wait," Ken interrupted. "You just said it was according to our obedience. Isn't that what I've been saying in the first place?"

"But I also mentioned that God gives according to what is in our best interest," Bishop North added.

The words "best interest" sent Ken thinking back to their earlier conversations. "So are you saying it is according to God's grace that He gives blessings?"

"To a large degree, yes," the bishop said, "But we have to add one more idea to that."

"What's that?"

"It is God's nature to be good to us, His children. Just as we, as parents, want good things for our children. But there is a difference in that He is a wise giver."

"What do you mean?" Ken asked.

"Over the years, my kids have asked for some pretty outrageous things. Even the proverbial pony," the bishop added with a grin. "But I haven't always given them what they wanted, even when I could. It would be unwise and not in their best interests to give to them without conditions or judgment on abilities and trustworthiness. Likewise, God does not give indiscriminately. He is a wise giver. Ken, have you ever had clients who seemed to have the problem of giving their kids too much?"

"Yes," Ken replied. "I've seen parents who have worked hard and grown rich and then lavish their children with money. And the money, in turn, ruined the kids."

"I have a friend who was born into tremendous wealth," Bishop explained. "He has done well, and is a good person, but I'm sure that if *I* were born into such a condition, much of the good that is in me wouldn't be there. I would have missed out on some character development and would not have learned to exercise and grow in certain areas. My difficulties have helped me grow. Still Ken, how many of us, if we were offered the trial of great wealth, wouldn't take it?"

"Maybe I would take the risk for a while." Ken smiled as he offered his hand into the air.

"So God doesn't give us according to what we want," the bishop again concluded, "but according to what is best for us. He gives us those things that will help us grow and become more like Him."

"There is a scripture that shows this is how God gives to us," Bishop North said as he moved the pages in his scriptures. "In Mosiah 4:21, King Benjamin is giving an example of how we should give to those in need the same way the Lord gives to—or blesses—us. It says:

> And now, if God, who has created you, on whom you are dependent for your lives and for all that ye have and are, doth grant unto you whatsoever ye ask that is right, in faith, believing that ye shall receive, O then, how ye ought to impart of the substance that ye have one to another.

"Prior to that verse, he spoke about how we should help those in need. But not according to what the poor have earned with us, but to be good—to be merciful—as God is merciful to us. In other words, God gives us according to what is *right* and good for us. He gives what is in our best interest just as we should give to those in need.

Ken suddenly sat back as a pain and heaviness came over his face. "How is my son nearly drowning in my best interest or what is right for me?"

"Ken," Bishop finally said after waiting and studying Ken's face, "God didn't cause that accident. It was part of this fallen world we live in. We really need to talk more about this. But I do want you to understand that even through this tragedy, God has a blessing prepared for you and your family. Placed before you is an opportunity to progress and grow more like the Savior than at probably any other time in your life. It's up to you to determine the growth."

"One last try to make sure I understand," Ken said soberly. "I'm no scripture scholar, but everywhere in the Book of Mormon, it says that if you keep the commandments, you'll prosper in the land. To me that kind of sounds like if I do commandment 'X', I'm bound to get blessing 'Z'."

"You would be right," Bishop North replied. "But not because you wrestled God's hand behind His back. God is bound in the same sense as a good father is bound to care for his children. And Ken, how does God know if we are ready for a particular blessing? By what we ask for?"

"Actions speak louder than words," Ken answered. "Our works show God how much He can trust us."

"Exactly, Ken. When we do well with the commandments and responsibilities we are given, God will then want to give us more freedoms and blessings. Our keeping of the commandments shows God we are ready for those things. Yet God always has our best interest in mind."

Ken sighed as he looked up at the ceiling. "Talking about these things sometimes brings out the lawyer in me. I don't give up easily. I do have another concern—a quick one," Ken added.

"Please," Bishop North said. "Go ahead."

"I know when you were teaching us about grace the other night, you were talking about how we should show kindness beyond what we think others deserve. I sort of get that. But in the context of salvation, I thought of it differently."

"How's that?" Bishop asked.

Ken grabbed a pad of notebook paper and a pen standing in a cup on the desk. "I thought of it this way. Because we sin, we have fallen from God's presence. So we are trying to get from where we are down here, to where He is up there. Doing good gets us up part of the way back. But we can never be good enough in this life to get back on our own. So God makes up the difference, and that is His grace," Ken said as he dropped the pen in the cup and slid the drawing over for the bishop to see.

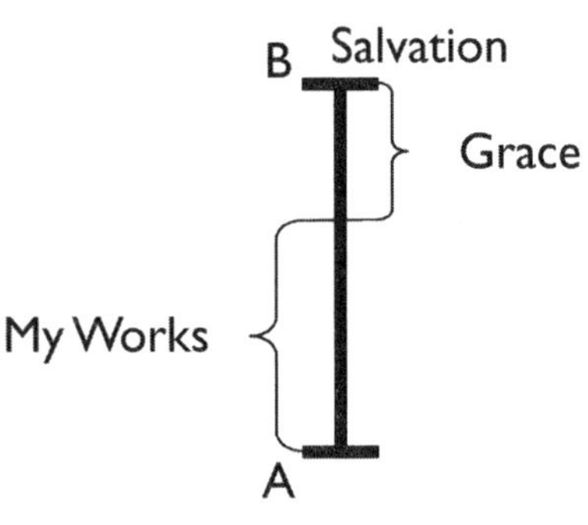

"It's a great analogy. And it even makes a lot of sense. But it has a big problem," Bishop North said. "The scriptures teach that it just does not work this way."

"You're going to need

to show me," Ken said, looking concerned.

"I know," Bishop North said as he started to open up his scriptures again. "But before the scriptures, here is the principle. The problem with returning ourselves back to our Heavenly Father is not the lack of righteousness. It is sin. There are quite a few scriptures, but here is one that comes to mind at the moment. Here in Luke seventeen, Jesus gives a comparison. In the comparison, God is like the master and we are like the servants. He says:

> But which of you, having a servant plowing or feeding cattle, will say unto him by and by, when he is come from the field, Go and sit down to meat?
>
> And will not rather say unto him, Make ready wherewith I may sup, and gird thyself, and serve me, till I have eaten and drunken; and afterward thou shalt eat and drink?
>
> Doth he thank that servant because he did the things that were commanded him? I trow not.
>
> So likewise ye, when ye shall have done all those things which are commanded you, say, We are unprofitable servants: we have done that which was our duty to do.

"In other words, back then when a master told his servant to do the chores, did he afterwards thank him? No, because the servant was only doing what he was supposed to do in the first place. Likewise, when we choose the right, we don't get any special credit from it toward our salvation, because choosing the right is what we were supposed to do in the first place. Judgment day is not going to be an opening of the books and looking at how many plus marks are by your name, versus how many minus signs; good deeds canceling out bad deeds. Righteousness doesn't counterbalance for our sins. Sin digs our hole deeper, but righteousness, of itself, cannot get us out of the hole we make. Doing what we should only keeps the hole from getting any deeper."

"Then why be good at all?" Ken replied, obviously looking frustrated.

"Order up," Erica called from outside the office.

"Thanks, Erica," Bishop North called back.

"You need to get those sandwiches and drinks back to your office, Ken," Bishop said as the two men stood up. "We will talk later about why good works are essential. I also want you to think about what we've talked about. You do some searching and pondering on your own."

"That would be good," Ken replied. "I'll email you later."

"And Ken," Bishop said, stopping him by the door by placing his hand on Ken's shoulder. "Will you stay away from that woman? Will you do whatever it takes?"

"I will," Ken said, pausing longer to reply than expected. Then Ken nodded his head to confirm his words.

As Ken drove away from the bakery he looked at his watch, realizing that when you offer to get lunch for your office, it isn't nice to be late. As Ken made his way at a faster pace now, he thought about the discussion with his bishop. "Good deeds don't make up for bad? Righteousness doesn't cancel out bad? That makes no sense at all," Ken said out loud.

Suddenly Ken saw the dreaded flashing blue and red lights in his rearview mirror. "Crud!" he exclaimed as he looked down at his speedometer and then started to pull over to the side.

"Good afternoon, officer."

"Do you know what your speed was?" the officer asked, ignoring his greeting.

"I'm sure I was speeding a bit."

"Can I see your license and registration?"

"Sure," Ken said as he fished for his wallet and looked in the glove compartment. As the officer walked back to his squad car, Ken slowly blew out air, trying to keep down his frustration. As he waited, an idea came into Ken's mind. *Good has to count for something.* Ken smiled as he thought of a way out of the ticket.

"I clocked you going thirteen over the speed limit," the officer said as he handed Ken his license and registration back.

"Officer, you're right," Ken started. "I really was speeding. But I think when you take into consideration all my good driving, you won't give me the ticket."

The officer paused with a slightly amused look on his face at this novel approach to getting out of a ticket. "Why won't I?"

"You see, officer, I've been a much better driver today than bad. Back there I came to a complete stop at two stop signs and waited at the red light. I have stayed in my lane and used my blinker when changing lanes. I have current licensing and registration. I slowed down to fifteen miles an hour through the school zone back there. Surely all that good driving outweighs my going a few miles over the speed limit just now."

"I'm glad you've been a responsible driver," the officer started saying with a laugh.

"Much more good driving than bad," Ken added.

"I'm sure that might be true. But that doesn't change that you broke the law," the officer replied as he wrote a new note on his clipboard. "But tell you what, for making me laugh, I'll reduce it to five over. Remember the speed limit is forty on this street."

"Thank you, officer," Ken said as the officer handed him the ticket and walked back to his patrol car.

chapter nine

INJUSTICE

Anna decided to stop at a pharmacy to pick up something she had put off for a couple of weeks. *Love Mitch like the Savior loves people,* Anna said in her mind as she drove away from the store, reviewing and thinking of ways to apply what she had learned in the bishop's office the other night. *Be kinder to him than what he deserves.* She thought about what Mitch had said to her and the names he called her when she invited him to come visit with the bishop. The sting wasn't as great as when he started calling her names when they were first married.

As Anna quietly entered the back door to the apartment, she could hear that her daughter Caitlin was still awake. She could also see the light from the TV reflecting on the back wall, making it clear that Mitch had neglected putting their daughter down and was just watching TV.

Grace will change everything, she thought again with some doubt as she moved closer to the room where her husband and daughter were.

"Caitlin, get off my legs," Mitch said as he physically moved her down from his legs, which were propped up on a stool in front of the TV. Taking little notice of the rebuke, Caitlin bounced down and then started to jump up and down while Mitch continued to watch his TV show.

As Anna secretly observed the situation, she wondered how she could show grace in this situation. *Oh, you're such a wonderful husband and thanks for all you do,* she thought sarcastically as she stood out of sight, behind the two.

"Move out of the way," Mitch said halfheartedly as Caitlin continued to bounce in and out of the view of the TV screen. "Caitlin! Quit acting stupid and get out of the way."

"Don't call her stupid!" Anna demanded forcefully as she came from the back to stand at their side.

"Mommy's home!" Caitlin shouted as she ran over and hugged one of Anna's legs.

"Don't you ever call her stupid or any other name again!" Anna said as she put one hand on her daughter's head and pointed a finger at Mitch with the other.

"Relax," Mitch defended. "It's no big deal. Is this what you learned when you went to the bishop's office: to come home and start screaming at everyone?"

"I should start screaming," Anna said in a slightly lower voice. "Calling your daughter names is a big deal."

"What? I call you stupid all the time," Mitch said defiantly.

"I know, and she isn't going to be treated the way you have treated me. Is that clear?" Anna was slightly surprised with how forcefully her words were coming out. Perhaps this was the most forceful she had ever been with Mitch, and for once he said nothing. He continued to scowl, got up, and walked away to their bedroom upstairs.

"Let's go to bed, honey," Anna said as she pulled Caitlin closer to her and tried to recompose herself. As usual, Anna and Mitch stayed far from each other after their fight, often with the hope that things would cool down the next day and not be so bad. Yet Anna seethed in her anger. She knew she would not allow her daughter to go through the same verbal abuse and hurtful language that she had endured from Mitch. That same night, Anna sat down at the computer and started an email to the bishop.

> It won't work for us!
> We are too far gone.
> Grace doesn't work in our situation.

After every line, Anna would quickly backspace over the words to remove what she had written. Finally she decided on a few thoughts to send:

Bishop,

You said that grace changes everything. Our marriage and family desperately needs to change, but I don't get it. You said showing grace would transform everything, but how? How will it change anything? I want to believe. I felt the Spirit when you were talking about giving grace to others. But I've also been looking at the situation I'm in. It seems that if I offer Mitch grace, he would just become a bigger jerk and I would become a bigger victim to his behavior. I know I should just trust in grace, but I need to see some light at the end of the tunnel.

How will grace change anything? How could it change us?

Anna

Bishop North didn't get the email until the next day after work. Instead of quickly responding, he pondered as he repeated her question, *How will grace change anything?*

"How was work?" Eden asked when she saw her husband come into the kitchen while she was breaking lettuce for a dinner salad.

"It was okay," Bishop North signed back and then gave his wife a gentle hug. He then left her side and dropped into the armchair in the family room, which was just off the kitchen.

Eden could see the burden in her husband's expression. She stopped making the salad and sat down on the ottoman in front of the armchair where her husband was. Instead of saying anything, she simply looked at him and, with her eyes, invited him to share what was bothering him.

"How does grace change people's lives?" he finally signed and spoke to her.

"What do you mean?" she asked, knowing there was more behind the question.

"You know I've been working with a group of members in the ward," he signed. "And I've been trying to express to them how showing grace to each other will heal their hearts and change their relationships. Then one of them emailed me asking how grace will change anything. I'm not sure I know how to answer her. I know grace changes everything. It's changed everything in my life. But how does grace do that?"

The two sat there pondering. Then Eden stood. Bishop North looked up, surprised to think that she would just leave. But instead, she plopped down on his lap. "Do you love me?" she asked as she playfully poked him with her finger.

"Always," he responded with sincerity and a look that let her know he meant it.

"Did you love me before my brain tumor?" Eden asked.

"Of course," he replied, wondering why she would even be asking such a question.

"Did your love change?" Eden continued in her questioning.

"I don't know if the tumor has had much to do with it, but I have grown to love you more and more," he signed back and spoke.

"But think hard," she said earnestly. "Did the whole experience with the cancer and losing my hearing increase your love for me in any way?"

Bishop North thought back to that time period: the pleading prayers, the surgeries, learning how to sign, the extra care and concern.

"You were wonderful to me," Eden continued. "Not that you were bad before or since, but with all the incredible sacrifice and care you gave to me at that time, did it increase your love for me in any way?"

Bishop North only nodded his head and looked in his wife's eyes, her tears brimming on the edges.

"The grace and goodness you showed me not only helped me," Eden said. "But it changed you. Sacrifice for someone increases love for that person."

"Wow," the bishop signed. "So it's not just 'I love you for all you do for me,' but it's also 'I love you because of *all I do* for you.' "

"Right," Eden said. "Like with our kids. Perhaps the reason we love them so much isn't what they do for us, but what we do for them. And the more we do for them, the more our love for them grows."

"I'm a lucky man," Bishop North said.

"You really are." Eden smiled as she snuggled deeper into his arms.

"Come in," Bishop North said as he invited Anna into his office at the church.

"Sorry about having to talk to me again," Anna said as she came in, holding her daughter's hand. "You must be starting to feel like you live in this office."

"It's not a bad place," Bishop said candidly as he opened his desk drawer and found a coloring book and crayons. "Do you think you can color this picture for me?" Bishop North asked Caitlin, who enthusiastically agreed and started on the picture.

"I tried and couldn't do it," Anna said, getting right to the point of her frustration. "With this whole grace thing, I was up half the night thinking about it. I'm okay with Mitch getting better than what he deserves. I even want him to have that grace."

"Then what's the problem, Anna?" Bishop asked.

"It's not fair to me," Anna said more forcefully than she intended. Fairness meant a lot to Anna. It was part of her competitive nature. When playing board games, she wanted to win more than anyone. Likewise, nothing was more infuriating to her than if someone cheated or wasn't playing by the rules. To her, it wasn't a joke; it was personal.

"What do you mean?" Bishop North replied.

"What about me? What about what I deserve? I'm the one getting the bad deal and showing this goodness and loving him like that. It makes what I am owed even worse. I think about how it would be if I were to treat Mitch the way you are asking, and then I imagine the future and what would be a sad life, always giving more than the other, always getting the short end of things. Bishop, I don't want the life of a martyr."

"Anna, I would never want you to have a sad life, and God certainly wouldn't want that either. In fact, living this way will give you a more happy and blessed life. You would find more joy than I'm sure you have had in a long time."

"But I would feel like I was getting robbed, always giving and never receiving. Don't I deserve a little happiness and kindness?"

"Absolutely, Anna," Bishop replied.

"Then how can that be if I were to be living the way you are saying? I don't see the justice in it."

"You're right, Anna," Bishop confirmed. "Think back to when we talked about the Israelites. They had injustice in Egypt, the law of Moses gave them justice, and then Jesus showed them the even higher way of grace."[1]

"But to the one giving the grace and goodness, it feels more like injustice," Anna objected.

"Anna, think over your life and all that you have been given," Bishop North said. "Has God been better to you than what you have done for Him or what the Lord would have owed you?"

"Yes. Far better," Anna replied after some thought. "But Mitch hasn't."

"Then this is your chance to give a little back. Not because Mitch has been so good to you, but because God has. Whatever you give more to Mitch than what is fair, God will make up the difference. And trust me, Anna, God will never allow Himself to get into debt to you.[2] God gives to us graciously. Now He wants us to go and do the same."[3]

Anna just stared at Bishop North and sighed. "It must get frustrating trying to get a point across to a person like me."

"What do you mean?" he asked with a smile.

"It still feels like it would be a life of being taken advantage of. Like I said, 'the life of a martyr.' "

"Grace changes everything, Anna," Bishop North said with a smile of hope. "You show grace to Mitch, and I believe you'll see it changing him."

"I guess this is my question I asked through email earlier," Anna said. "How does grace change things?"

"In two ways: it changes the person who is touched by the grace, and it changes the person who extends the grace. First, let's look at how it changes the person who receives the grace from another. Anna, have you ever been in traffic and someone intentionally was kind and considerate?

"Sure."

"Did you then feel a bit more inclined not just to show kindness to the driver who let you in, but to show extra courtesy to other drivers?"

"That has happened to me," Anna said as she thought about rush-hour traffic that morning and a man that had let her in when she realized, too late, that her lane on the freeway was ending. "It was easier to show kindness to everyone driving."

"So you show that extra goodness for Mitch, and you will see it changing the way he treats you. Grace begets grace. It's like that scripture we read the other day, 'Love your enemies, bless them that curse you, do good to them that hate you, and pray for them which despitefully use you and persecute you.' I'm sure you don't think of Mitch as your enemy. And so doesn't that give you all the more reason to show him that extra goodness?"

"You're right," Anna said.

"Jesus mentioned praying there," Bishop North pointed out. "Do you pray for Mitch often?"

"I used to; quite often," Anna said after some thought. A long time ago, when Anna was in Young Women, someone had taught her that she should pray for her future spouse. The idea struck her with power. She got in the habit of praying each night for this unknown young man who would one day be her husband. She remembered praying that he would be able to resist the temptations of the world and live worthy to serve a full-time mission, and that they would find each other. Now she thought it strange that she had prayed for Mitch before they met and she rarely prayed for him now that he was her husband.

"Mitch needs your prayers as much now as ever before," Bishop North said. "Will you start praying for him again?"

Just as Anna was about to agree, a thought quickly crossed Anna's mind. *Bet you he's never prayed for me.* But Anna quickly bit her bottom lip, realizing how petty she had become with Mitch. "I will, Bishop."

"Showing grace to others truly changes people," Bishop North started. "But perhaps what is more incredible is what it does to the one showing the grace. Do you remember your brother's Mustang?"

"How could I forget?" Anna said, thinking back. Anna had a younger brother, Chuck, who Bishop North worked with in Young Men's before he became bishop. Chuck had inherited a 1965 Ford Mustang from their father.

"Do you remember how much effort he put into that car?" Bishop asked.

"He was always working on it," Anna said as she thought back to how Chuck was constantly fixing, cleaning, upgrading, replacing, or doing something with it. "And every paycheck from his job seemed to go into that car in some way. He loved that car."

"Anna, why did Chuck love his car so much?"

"I have no idea," Anna replied. "I thought the car was cool, but not that cool."

"Do you think it might have had something to do with how much effort and sacrifice he was putting into it?"

"What do you mean?" Anna asked. "I would hate a car that was so much trouble."

"Think of how people appreciate things they earn themselves, rather than what is just given them. The car was cool, but I'm sure that if you or I were just given the car in mint condition, we wouldn't appreciate it as much. Perhaps the reason your brother loved the car so much was because of all he put into it. The more he sacrificed for the car, the more he loved it.

"Likewise with your daughter, Caitlin," Bishop North said as he pointed over to Anna's daughter coloring. "Part of the reason you love her so much is because of all you do for her. People love what they invest themselves into."

"Does this explain about the Savior's love too?" Anna asked.

"Go on with your thought," Bishop North encouraged.

"I'm sure the Savior loved us before He suffered and died for us," Anna said, drawing out her thought slowly. "But maybe the Lord's love is so great for us because of all He suffered and sacrificed for us. No one has ever suffered more for another than the Savior for us. So maybe this partly explains why the Lord's love exceeds all other forms of love."

"You're right on, Anna," Bishop agreed. "And it also works the other way with our relationship with the Savior. If we sacrifice and show grace toward others, we also come to know the Savior better. We have the 'fellowship of his sufferings.'[4] We will come to understand His love for us a little better."

"You know, Bishop," Anna started to say while her eyes turned toward the window, a faraway look on her face, "When Mitch and I were dating, I think I tried much harder. I wanted him to like me so badly that I was thoughtful and always trying. Maybe that is partly why I loved him so much more in the beginning."

"I'm sure it was," Bishop North confirmed with encouragement. "Now you need to do it again. Look for something good in Mitch and write him a note expressing your appreciation for that. If you do that, and can keep your pride out of the way, you'll find yourself loving him more as you are writing that note. Will you try it?"

"I bet you do things like that all the time," Anna said rather than accepting the commitment. "I love your wife. Eden is one of the most incredible people I've ever met. You married the right person. But I'm honestly wondering if I did."

"Let me make sure I understand," Bishop said. "You are wondering if you married the right person. 'Mr. Right.' *'Your one and only.'* "

"I really do wonder that," Anna defended. "I think I acted too quickly, and there was a lot I didn't see in him at first. It hasn't been the happy life I imagined. My point is, if he's not the right one, wouldn't showing all this grace and everything be for nothing?"

"Can I share another scripture with you about a woman who perhaps saw things in the same way, with relationships?" Bishop asked. "You're not getting sick of the scriptures, are you?"

"No," Anna replied. "In fact, sometimes it's easier to take these points from the scriptures rather than just what my bishop is saying."

"Thanks," Bishop North said with a laugh as he started to turn the pages of his scriptures. "That's just how it should be."

"I'm also wondering what woman in the scriptures you are talking about," Anna said.

"It's in John chapter 4," Bishop North replied. "The woman at the well was thirsting for more than just water. Jesus told her:

> But whosoever drinketh of the water that I shall give him shall never thirst; but the water that I shall give him shall be in him a well of water springing up into everlasting life.

"The woman wasn't gullible, thinking this stranger really had some magic water. She knew Jesus was speaking in metaphor, like Middle Eastern people do. She said, 'Sir, give me this water, that I thirst not, neither come hither to draw.' This woman had a great thirst that the world had never quenched. Jesus immediately got to the point by asking her to get her husband. She said she didn't have one, to which Jesus said,

> Thou hast well said, I have no husband:
> For thou hast had five husbands; and he whom thou now hast is not thy husband: in that saidst thou truly.

"Similar to many men and women today, this woman had hopped from one relationship to another. Always hoping to find that man who would make her happy.

"Our society teaches the same thing," Bishop went on. "Young girls are taught to find their Prince Charming who will make all of their dreams come true. In other words, some think that happiness is finding the right person who will make them happy. People who hold on to this expectation in relationships are always disappointed."

"What's wrong with finding the right person?" Anna objected.

"It's in the story," Bishop replied. "This woman had looked for fulfillment by placing all of her expectations for happiness on different men. When those men failed her—and people will always fail to be perfect—then she would jump into another relationship. But what the woman ultimately found that filled her thirst was the Savior. A spouse cannot make us happy. We're always going to resent a spouse who we place that kind of expectation on. Only having the proper relationship with God can bring true peace and happiness in this world. Mitch can't fill the empty places in your life. God never intended our spouses to be the source of our entire fulfillment. He has reserved that place in our lives for Himself. If you are putting Mitch in the place where God should be in your life, you'll always be frustrated with him, and he'll fail to meet your expectations. God gave Adam his wife, Eve, who was just right for him. But she was not to take the place of God in Adam's life."

"I'm a little surprised by what you're saying," Anna said. "Especially when I look at you and your wife, Eden. It's easy to see you're both incredibly in love with each other. I could only hope to have something like you two have."

"You're right," Bishop North said. "I love her with all of my heart. I feel like the most blessed man on earth. But God being the center of our relationship is the source of our happiness together. He has shown us how to forgive and how to show goodness to each other, even when the other might not necessarily deserve it. The Lord has made our relationship wonderful. That is what God wants to do now for you and Mitch."

Anna wondered if that was possible. "I want what you have, and I want to have our relationship like you're saying, Bishop, but

I am not sure where to start."

"That's what we have been talking about," Bishop said. "Show him goodness beyond what he deserves or has merited. Be good to him. Simply love him."

"Simply love him," Anna repeated softly as she looked down. "I'm honestly not sure I do love him anymore. It feels like the love's gone."

"Weaved in what you just said is another false idea from our society," Bishop North said with a sigh. "People talk about falling in and out of love like it is a passive experience that just happens to us. As if love is a magical state of mind that we have no control over. It's there, and then it's gone. The scriptures talk of love quite differently. In the scriptures, love is not something you feel as much as something you do. In the Bible, marriages were usually arranged. When Isaac's marriage was arranged, he met Rebekah, and it says, 'Isaac . . . took Rebekah, and she became his wife; and he loved her.' There you get the idea that love was an action of Isaac's toward his wife. It wasn't *love*, then *marriage*. They married first and then showed love to each other. In the Doctrine and Covenants the Lord says, 'Thou shalt love thy wife with all thy heart, and shalt cleave unto her and none else.' It didn't say to 'be in love with your wife' but to love her. The logic is that we will *be* in love with those to whom we show love.

"So if I just do it, I will feel it? But love isn't like that," Anna objected. "You can't show it if you don't feel it."

"Anna, did you get good grades?"

"Close to straight As," Anna replied.

"I thought so," Bishop congratulated. "Did you always feel like doing your homework?"

"Not usually," Anna replied.

"Then why did you do something you didn't feel like doing?"

"I wanted good grades," Anna replied. "I did it because it was important."

"Your marriage is important," Bishop stated. "You will not always feel like being kind or good to Mitch. But marriage is important. Just like your homework, show him goodness even when you don't feel like it. Even when you're not feeling any love at that particular moment. Strangely, you'll find that love is not so much a matter of how he is to you, but rather how you are to him.

Show it, and you'll feel it."

NOTES

1. See John 1:17.
2. For insights on how the Lord will never let himself get in debt to us, see Mosiah 2:23–24.
3. In 1 Corinthians 6:7, Paul spoke to members of the church who were suing each other in court, saying, "Why do ye not rather take wrong? why do ye not rather suffer yourselves to be defrauded?" A similar idea is in Matthew 10:8, where the Lord teaches, "Freely ye have received, freely give."
4. See Philippians 3:10.

chapter ten

GOOD WORKS

"Your experience with the police officer made me laugh," the bishop started in reply to an email Ken had written him about the officer and also how he had been careful to stay clear of the woman at work. "I've also been thinking that we needed to talk more about what part good works plays in our salvation. I've looked up a few scriptures, so let's look at that more carefully.

"In your analogy, you brought up the idea that our good works (or our merits) get us part of the way back to heaven and then grace (the Lord's merits) makes up the difference. The terms *merit* or *merits* only come up eight times in scripture. Seven of them are in the context of salvation, and all but one of them are in the Book of Mormon. Here are four of them. Look at what role it says our merits have and the role of Christ's merits.

> And since man had fallen he *could not merit anything of himself*; but the sufferings and death of Christ atone for their sins, through faith and repentance, and so forth. (Alma 22:14, emphasis added)

> Wherefore, how great the importance to make these things known unto the inhabitants of the earth, that they may know that there is no flesh that can dwell in the presence of God, *save it be through the merits, and mercy, and grace of the Holy Messiah*, who layeth down his life according to the flesh,

> and taketh it again by the power of the Spirit, that he may bring to pass the resurrection of the dead, being the first that should rise. (2 Nephi 2:8, emphasis added)

> And now, my beloved brethren, after ye have gotten into this strait and narrow path, I would ask if all is done? Behold, I say unto you, Nay; for ye have not come thus far save it were by the word of Christ with unshaken faith in him, *relying wholly upon the merits of him who is mighty to save.* (2 Nephi 31:19, emphasis added)

> And after they had been received unto baptism, and were wrought upon and cleansed by the power of the Holy Ghost, they were numbered among the people of the church of Christ; and their names were taken, that they might be remembered and nourished by the good word of God, to keep them in the right way, to keep them continually watchful unto prayer, *relying alone upon the merits of Christ,* who was the author and the finisher of their faith. (Moroni 6:4, emphasis added)

Never do the verses talk about relying partially on our merits. Always it is completely His merits. And it seems we can't merit anything because of our fallen state.

There are other scriptures that suggest the same thing. When Amulek was teaching a group of Nephites, he said:

> Yea, I would that ye would come forth and harden not your hearts any longer; for behold, *now is the time and the day of your salvation*; and therefore, if ye will repent and harden not your hearts, immediately shall the great plan of redemption be brought about unto you. (Alma 34:31, emphasis added)

Notice that salvation was offered to them right there—that day. Not "Start changing your lives, repent, make up for what you have done wrong, and do good, and in the future you might be able to have salvation." When one is repentant and has entered into covenants with God and his course is on the right path, salvation is his to enjoy now.[1]

In Ezekiel 18 it talks about how when a person who may have been wicked all his life turns from his sins to righteousness, all his wickedness is forgotten. Likewise, when a righteous person (one who might have accrued lots of good works) turns away to wickedness, all his righteousness (merits) are forgotten. In verse 25 it even mentions how the Israelites, who felt salvation was merited, would say that this wasn't fair.

The parable of the laborers in Matthew 20:1–15 does the same thing. There it says:

> For the kingdom of heaven is like unto a man that is an householder, which went out early in the morning to hire labourers into his vineyard.
>
> And when he had agreed with the labourers for a penny a day, he sent them into his vineyard.
>
> And he went out about the third hour, and saw others standing idle in the marketplace,
>
> And said unto them; Go ye also into the vineyard, and whatsoever is right I will give you. And they went their way.
>
> Again he went out about the sixth and ninth hour, and did likewise.
>
> And about the eleventh hour he went out, and found others standing idle, and saith unto them, Why stand ye here all the day idle?
>
> They say unto him, Because no man hath hired us. He saith unto them, Go ye also into the vineyard; and whatsoever is right, that shall ye receive.
>
> So when even was come, the lord of the vineyard saith unto his steward, Call the labourers, and give them their hire, beginning from the last unto the first.
>
> And when they came that were hired about the eleventh hour, they received every man a penny.
>
> But when the first came, they supposed that they should have received more; and they likewise received every man a penny.
>
> And when they had received it, they murmured against the goodman of the house,
>
> Saying, These last have wrought but one hour, and thou hast made them equal unto us, which have borne the burden and heat of the day.
>
> But he answered one of them, and said, Friend, I do thee no wrong: didst not thou agree with me for a penny?
>
> Take that thine is, and go thy way: I will give unto this last, even as unto thee.
>
> Is it not lawful for me to do what I will with mine own? Is thine eye evil, because I am good?

Some laborers worked for twelve hours while others worked for just one hour. Yet they all received the same reward. One of the points Jesus was trying to make about some working more in the parable and others working less, is that salvation is based on His merits. Not our merits.

Speaking about salvation, the Apostle Paul put it simply:

> And if by grace, then is it no more of works: otherwise grace is no more grace. But if it be of works, then is it no more grace: otherwise work is no more work. (Romans 11:6)

In other words, salvation is either by Christ's merits (grace) or our merits (works), but it can't be both.[2] Paul also said in Ephesians 2:8–9:

> For by grace are ye saved through faith; and that not of yourselves: it is the gift of God:
>
> Not of works, lest any man should boast.

What I find most striking about this verse is that there is no Joseph Smith translation. Surely the Prophet would not have simply overlooked this common verse. But instead the Lord wanted his prophet to let the verse, and its natural meaning, stand as it reads.[3]

There are many other scriptures, but D&C 45:3–5 is where the Lord gives us a glimpse into how Jesus mediates for us before the Father. It says:

> Listen to him who is the advocate with the Father, who is pleading your cause before him—
>
> Saying: Father, behold the sufferings and death of him who did no sin, in whom thou wast well pleased; behold the blood of thy Son which was shed, the blood of him whom thou gavest that thyself might be glorified;
>
> Wherefore, Father, spare these my brethren that believe on my name, that they may come unto me and have everlasting life.

Notice that prior to the Lord saying "Wherefore, Father, spare these brethren," he does not read our résumé of good works or catalog all of our righteousness. The Savior only mentions His own merits by which we should be spared.

Last, the scriptures always speak of salvation as a gift (D&C 14:7). So the question becomes, if a person pays for a gift they receive, is it really a gift? For instance, imagine that a man says, "I need a pencil." A second man says, "Here's a pencil; you can have it. My gift to you." The first man replies, "Thank you, here is a quarter." If it was a gift, will the first man accept the money? Thus, the Lord teaches us that "Salvation is free" (2 Nephi 2:4; 2 Nephi 26:27).

Well, Ken, this should be enough for tonight. It's late, and I should be going to bed. Did these scriptures help? I bet you are wondering what role our works play.

Bishop Stuart North

The next day Ken replied to the email:

Your list and your knowledge of the scriptures are impressive. I also tried to look for scriptures that say it is by works and came up with a couple. But in light of the scriptures you shared, I won't go into those.

You're right in that I really want to know what role works play. It almost makes me think, "Why work at all?" Also, it has me wondering: if our works are not saving us, and it is all by Christ's merits, then on what basis does the Lord save one person to celestial glory and not another? Why doesn't He just save everyone?

Ken Richards

Later Bishop North replied:

Hello Ken,

Don't be too impressed. It's a lot easier to answer someone when you can sit down at the computer and research things out. Your questions were right on target. Maybe we can answer both questions at the same time. By looking at the role good works play, we can also see why God brings some into celestial glory, but not others.

But before that, the first point that I must say is that good works are absolutely essential to salvation. Without them, no one would be saved. Yet they, of themselves, can't save us or merit our salvation. Here are a few reasons that works are so imperative to our salvation.

The first is that good works show the true faith and desires of our hearts. If I were to randomly find a hundred people and ask each if they wanted to go to heaven (assuming they all even believed in the concept of heaven), how many do you think would say they want to go? I would bet that most everyone would say they wanted heaven. If we imagine heaven as lounging on a celestial beach with angelic beings serving us tropical drinks, it seems to be the natural choice for most everyone.

But what if celestial glory were far different? Would all really like the lifestyle of exaltation? On my bulletin board I have a quote by Marion G. Romney that says:

> Service is not something we endure on this earth so we can earn the right to live in the celestial kingdom. Service is the very fiber of which an exalted life in the celestial kingdom is made.[4]

In other words, service is a central characteristic of heaven. It is the work and the glory of God to bring to pass our immortality and eternal life. God loves us so much that He puts unbelievable amounts of care and effort into bringing us back. Heaven is for those who want to become like God the Father and His Son Jesus Christ, and if They are all about service, then celestial glory, for us, will be all about service.

So if a person didn't like to serve in this life (if they despised every service project and person in need), would they really want heavenly glory? Most all would say they want heaven, but maybe many don't really know what they want.

My point is that our works show God what we really want. Our actions, and not our words, show God our desires. But some might think that they want to go to heaven, most of all, because they want to avoid hell. But we learn in D&C 76:43 that our merciful Savior will "save all the works of his hand" in the sense that all will receive wonderful places of glory.[5] I used to wonder how it was that every knee would bow before the Lord one day. Aren't there some people who always think they deserve better than what they get? Well, perhaps God's way of fixing that is that He will graciously give everyone far better than he or she deserves. That is not to say that all will enjoy celestial glory, but they will get considerably better than they have merited. And our works and actions show what we really desire for the next life.

Another reason that good works are so essential is that they show that we're taking care of our end of the covenants. Through the ordinances, God has extended celestial glory to His children. Our end of the covenant is that we show our faith by always striving to follow Him.

A final reason that good works are so important is that they help us to become like Him. Exaltation is all about becoming like God. Living the commandments daily helps us to develop God-like attributes. Jesus is all-forgiving, wise, kind, merciful, selfless, humble, and every other attribute of perfection. God can see that exaltation will only be the best destination for those who are striving to acquire those attributes in this life. I think that Dallin H. Oaks put this whole matter about good works and their purpose perfectly when he said:

> The Final Judgment is not just an evaluation of a sum total of good and evil acts—what we have *done*. It is an acknowledgment of the final effect of our acts and thoughts—what we have *become*. It is not enough for anyone just to go through the motions. The commandments, ordinances, and covenants of the gospel are not a list of deposits required to be made in some heavenly account. The gospel of Jesus Christ is a plan that shows us how to become what our Heavenly Father desires us to become.[6]

Let me know what you think.
Bishop North

Ken later replied:

Bishop,

I want to agree with what you're teaching me about grace and salvation, and still, there is part of me that wants to disagree. Here is part of the reason I have had a distaste for the term "grace." In college I knew a guy who called himself a "born-again Christian." He said that on some date, he proclaimed Christ as his "personal Savior," and from that moment on, he was "saved." He said that in the instant he was "saved" he was forgiven of all sin (past, present, and future) and so no matter what he did, he was going to go to heaven. How he translated that idea to daily living is that he could commit any sin (and often did), and still he would not fall from grace. When I would ask him about good works, he would say that it was by grace, and not works, that he was saved. He also said, "once saved, always saved" and nothing could change that. So in college I would see him committing all sorts of sin with little concern. When I would mention it, he would just reply, "Saved by grace."

I hope we don't believe that, Bishop, and I'm sure we don't, but part of me thinks that we might be better off just thinking that we are saved by our works.

What say ye?

Ken

Bishop North replied.

Ken,

You're right. There's extreme danger in misunderstanding grace. Likewise, there's danger in misunderstanding the role of works. Let's first look at the danger of misunderstanding grace like your friend did.

I have also met people with that same understanding of grace and salvation. They see grace as a license to sin. Thankfully, I think few serious Christians see sin that way.

The biggest problem with those few, and their understanding of grace, is what they sandwich grace with. On one side of grace they have the doctrine of "eternal security," which is the "once saved, always saved" doctrine. What they don't understand is that God will never take away a person's agency to reject Him. And the pursuit of sin is the rejection of God and His salvation. The Lord tells us plainly in D&C 20:32 that people can "fall from grace." We believe we need to be continually trying to follow Christ in order to receive that ongoing grace that brings salvation. In the Topical Guide, there is a wonderful part titled "Grace, Man May Fall from" that makes it so clear how "eternal security" is a false doctrine. You should explore that in the Topical Guide sometime, if you're interested.

The second side of the false doctrine sandwich is what they believe to be necessary to receive that grace in their lives. Most believe you only need to confess Christ as your personal Savior. And since that is all that is necessary, they then believe that following Him is nice but not necessary. One of the classic scriptures they use to demonstrate this idea is Romans 10:9–10, 13. There it says:

> That if thou shalt confess with thy mouth the Lord Jesus, and shalt believe in thine heart that God hath raised him from the dead, thou shalt be saved.
>
> For with the heart man believeth unto righteousness; and with the mouth confession is made unto salvation. . . .
>
> For whosoever shall call upon the name of the Lord shall be saved.

It almost sounds like if you just believe a few details, and confess it, then you will be saved. But there are two details that often are missed. One is in the beginning of verse 10, "For with the heart man believeth unto righteousness." True belief always leads to righteousness (or good works). Whatever belief doesn't lead to righteousness is not the belief that leads to salvation. There can be no *faith* without *faithfulness*. For instance, if I said that I buried one million dollars in my backyard and whoever digs it up can have it, those who really believe will get their shovels and start to dig.

The other detail that some miss is the word "Lord" that is used. This is not just a trite title for Jesus Christ. Paul is expressing what position the Savior is to play in our lives. "Lord" means He is to be the one in authority in our lives, the Master of our choices, and we are to be His servants. If He is truly our Lord, wc will do what He commands of us. Any less dedication to the Savior will not lead to salvation.

Yet like you said earlier, if there is such a danger in misunderstanding grace in our salvation, isn't it safer to just believe salvation comes from our works?

There is also great danger in the opposite extreme. You said that maybe it was better to believe that we merit our salvation. If a person sees all of their blessings and even their salvation as a product of their own works alone, it will warp and pervert the way that person sees God and their discipleship. Here are the five dangers I see in believing that all is based on our works:

It takes our focus off of God when good things happen. If a person believes that all blessings come from his obedience, then when good things come along, instead of praising God for the blessings, he thinks to praise himself for the good works that must have led to the blessing. Instead of thanking God, he pats himself on the back, smiles, and ponders over how righteous he is for every good thing that comes along.

This could lead him to place his faith in himself (and his own good works) rather than placing his faith in Christ. Eventually, he might even imagine himself in heaven, boasting in himself and his own good works rather than in Christ who saved him by His good works. But in reality, there is only one who will be praised in that day. God always made it very clear to the Israelites that their blessings came because of God's goodness and not their own so that they would rely on and have faith in Him. A person's perception of how salvation is obtained affects the very nature of his faith in Jesus Christ. If we believe salvation is gained as a combination of our works and His grace, then faith is placed in our works rather than in Christ. That would even distract us from being true followers of Jesus Christ. It is important to believe in salvation resulting wholly from His merits because that belief immediately takes our focus off of us and places it on the Lord Jesus Christ, the author and finisher of our faith. Not "my part" and "your part" thinking but rather "partnership."

With the correct understanding, we will focus on being followers of Christ rather than our works and trying to reach some mythical level of righteousness where His grace can then kick in. I believe all of us can have a greater spiritual awakening when we no longer focus on our works being good enough but when we think more in terms of being His disciples and followers of Christ.

We blame God for all bad things. This is the second danger of believing we save ourselves by our own good works. If a person is living a fairly good life and believes that blessings come from obedience, then when life's difficulties come (and they always do), he will feel to blame God. "Couldn't an all-powerful God stop this tragedy from happening?"

People with this misunderstanding are always left wondering why good things happen to bad people and why bad things happen to good people. They want to think that "If I pay this offering, I'll increase my income" or "If I live this commandment,

I'll never get sick" or "If I do that, my children will never struggle or fall away." But the truth is that the payment of tithing doesn't ensure financial bliss, many people who live the Word of Wisdom have severe health problems, and many who have family scripture study and prayer have children who struggle also. Now don't get me wrong. Keeping the commandments and living the principles of the gospel will help us avoid great heaps of pain, suffering, and difficulties. Most often we are blessed financially, physically, and in every other way as we live the teachings of the Lord. But keeping the commandments is not like payment into a commandment 401K plan that brings us the equity to later procure the blessings of our choice.

To people with this misunderstanding, the world never seems fair. They constantly resent God, wondering, "Why is this happening to me?" and blame God for every perceived injustice. The truth is, this world isn't fair. This telestial world is fallen and cruel. It is the nature of this world we chose to come to so that we could grow. That is why we hope for a better world. If one believes that living the gospel should always bring a life of comfort, then one must also consider the lives of the great men and women of the scriptures. The prophets were exceptionally good men, yet it is perhaps impossible to find one who had an easy life: Joseph Smith, Abraham, Abinadi,[7]—even our Savior, who lived a perfect life and deserved the fewest difficulties, had the most. Ken, you said that you have had resentment toward your wife because of the accident. But have you also had resentment toward God for allowing this to happen?[8] This may be partly because of your understanding of how God gives salvation and blessings.

It causes us to judge others unrighteously. If we think that every positive thing happens because of some merit, and every negative thing because of some sin, then when bad things happen to others, we assume they must have done something to deserve it. Rather than having compassion, we wonder, "Master, who did sin, this man, or his parents, that he was born blind?" (see John 9:2). When someone's kids rebel or his car constantly breaks down or he struggles in poverty, we could be tempted to assume it is all because of his sins. Again, the truth is that this world is just fallen and bad things happen to good people.

Discouragement. If we think we earn our salvation, then we will always be discouraged when looking at ourselves and doubt that we are worthy enough to reach heaven. No matter the progress we make, celestial glory will always seem eternally out of reach. But a true understanding of how salvation is given replaces discouragement with hope. Here we see that if we are trying our best to follow the Savior and keep the covenants we have entered into, then we can expect eternal life.

Selfish giving. If we see God only being good to us according to what we have earned with Him (tit-for-tat giving), then how could we ever expect to do better with our fellow man than the way God has been with us? Rather than receiving back the prodigal son graciously, we would sit back and say to the prodigal, "I'll forgive you when you have earned back my love." We can't hope to treat people better than the way we see God treating us. If we see a God of only justice (giving to us only according to what we have earned or merited), then we will treat others likewise. If we see a God who is merciful and gracious, full of love and kindness, then we will try to do likewise. That is why it is so important to see the truly gracious way God loves and blesses us.

Ken, I've taken enough of your time, but do you feel better about the role of grace and works in our salvation? We must do our best to follow Christ, but in the end, His magnificent work in the garden and on the cross is what saves us. We must trust in Him by always trying to keep His commandments.

So now, what does this mean between you and your wife? Can you show her the same grace God is showing to you? Do you know how God wants you to love your wife?

Bishop North

As Ken finished reading the email and pondered, the light from the computer monitor reflected on his face. He thought about his typical view of God and how so much of what the bishop wrote was true. When good things had happened in his life, he had congratulated himself rather than giving the credit to God. He couldn't think of any success in life for which he had truly given God the credit.

Likewise, when those difficulties of life came, he had felt

resentment toward God rather than blaming himself. What responsibility did he share for their son's accident?

Ken could see that his contorted view of judgment had stretched toward the way he silently judged others.

NOTES

1. Brigham Young discussed the idea of enjoying our salvation while as mortals when he said, "I want present salvation. I preach, comparatively, but little about the eternities and Gods, and their wonderful works in eternity; and do not tell who first made them, nor how they were made; for I know nothing about that. Life is for us, and it is for us to receive it to-day, and not wait for the millenium. Let us take a course to be saved to-day, and, when evening comes, review the acts of the day, repent of our sins, if we have any to repent of, and say our prayers; then we can lie down and sleep in peace until the morning, arise with gratitude to God, commence the labours of another day, and strive to live the whole day to God and nobody else" (Brigham Young, in *Journal of Discourses* [London: Latter-day Saints' Book Depot, 1861], 8:124–25. See *Journal of Discourses* 1:131).
2. In Moses 7:59, Enoch further clarifies this thought when he says, "Thou hast made me, and given unto me a right to thy throne, and not of myself, but through thine own grace."
3. Many people counter Ephesians 2:8–9 with 2 Nephi 25:23. For a further analysis, see Stephen E. Robinson, *Believing Christ: The Parable of the Bicycle and Other Good News* (Salt Lake City: Deseret Book, 1992), 90.
4. Marion G. Romney, "The Celestial Nature of Self-reliance," *Ensign*, Nov. 1982, 91.
5. All of our Heavenly Father's children will receive places of glory except the sons of perdition, to whom God gives the agency to reject all He mercifully offers. See D&C 29:44.
6. Dallin H. Oaks, "The Challenge to Become," *Ensign*, Nov. 2000, 32.
7. Concerning the righteous suffering, Paul teaches in 2 Timothy 3:12, "Yea, and all that will live godly in Christ Jesus shall suffer persecution."
8. So how should Christ's followers attribute success or failure? The

enlightened view is when there is anything bad that happens, it is probably our own fault. And whatever is good comes from God's goodness and not our own righteousness. Bottom line: If good things happen to us, we should attribute it to God and give thanks to Him in all things. Think of it as being because of His goodness and mercy toward us unworthy creatures. For the Lord is far better to us than we will ever deserve. Likewise, when bad things happen to us, we shouldn't assume that it was God but rather that it is just part of the difficulties of this fallen world. That way, instead of blaming God, we will be led to fall on our knees and plead with God for help. Trials will then bring us closer to God rather than have us resent God.

chapter eleven

OBJECTIONS

Erica turned off the gigantic mixer and began the process of removing the fifty-pound mound of dough she had made.

"Good morning, Erica," Bishop North said as he came into his bakery. For years, he trusted only himself to get the bakery started up in the morning. But over the last year, Erica had proven herself responsible, dedicated, and able. Now Tuesdays and Thursdays were the mornings Erica would come in and get things going while Bishop North would come in the other four workdays.

"Good morning, Stuart," Erica said. It had been a few days since Bishop North had talked to Erica and the others about God's grace. Since then Erica had put some emotional distance between her and her boss. She had asked herself why she was treating her boss differently now but wasn't sure of the answer. Stuart North, now Bishop North, had become a father figure over the years. Strangely, Erica now felt some anger toward Bishop North, although she couldn't figure out why.

"So what did you think of the other night?" Bishop North asked as he put on his apron. Erica let silence be her answer as she cut and shaped pieces of dough.

"I don't understand why you invited me to your little meeting in the first place," Erica finally replied.

"I want you to know, Erica," Bishop North continued, "that I didn't ask you there because of you being an employee or me being your bishop. I really felt like you needed to hear about God and His grace."

"But why all the interest in me?" Erica asked forcefully as she worked the dough over. "Why do you care so much at all?"

"I don't think I ever told you about my mother, have I?" Bishop North eventually said after some reflective silence. "She had a tough life. I wasn't raised by her much, and I didn't come to know her till I was about your age. Her life had been rough. Maybe a lot like your life, in many ways." Bishop North paused occasionally as a look of pain seemed to settle over his expression. "I don't think she ever knew about God's love for her. I didn't really know about God either until someone reached out to me. A kind man showed me God's love, and it changed me. It changed my life. My mother died shortly after that. I wish someone had reached out to her and shown *her* God's love. Perhaps I want to share with you what I wasn't able to share with my mother."

Erica didn't say anything but was surprised by the expression on Bishop North's face as she occasionally glanced up.

"There is one more thing," Bishop North slowly added. "You and her share the same name of Erica. Since you came in the bakery that first day looking for a job, I've wanted to be the kind of good friend and strong support that man had been for me and I wish someone had been for my mother."

"You've always been a good friend to me," Erica said, finally stopping to rest. "You and your wife have been kind to me, and this job is about the only stable, good thing going on in my life. Thank you. But I just don't see God the way you do."

"What do you mean?" Bishop North asked.

"I want to believe in the loving, gracious God you talked about. But I just don't see it."

"I have an idea," Bishop North replied. "You think about any objections you have with God. We'll get things ready here quickly, and we should have about twenty minutes to talk about things before we open the front doors at ten."

"All right," Erica replied in a less than enthusiastic tone.

"Don't ponder so much that you burn or cut yourself," Bishop North said somewhat seriously.

As Erica worked, she did try to formulate what objections she had with God and why she felt He wasn't loving. As she thought, she realized that much of what she felt was a general feeling of resentment, but it was difficult to express.

"So what do you think, Erica?" Bishop North said as he bagged the last loaf of bread and tied it off.

"I don't think this is a good idea," Erica replied. "I don't think I should say everything I think, and I'm sure if I did, I would offend you."

"When you have a few years behind you like me, you have heard a lot. I'm pretty sure your thoughts won't be too far from what others have expressed as objections with God. I bet you we can resolve a few issues you have."

After debating in her mind whether she should share or not, she pulled out a spiral notebook from her bag. "I'm not good at speaking like you are," she said to Bishop North. "But I am a little better at expressing things on paper. I wrote down a few things during the break I took a little while ago."

"Let's hear it," Bishop North invited.

Just as Erica was about to read, she paused and wondered if she was now going to ruin some things between them. But her life crumbling apart was normal for her. She proceeded to read:

My Problems with God

If God is so great, why does He do so many terrible things? In the scriptures, if people are not doing things the way He wants them to, God floods the earth and kills them all. If He sees another city being wicked, He sends fire from heaven. How is that a loving God? Someone showed me that when the Israelites went into the Promised Land, they were commanded by God to kill every man, woman, and child. It's barbaric.

Is God any better now? Why does He allow all the pain and suffering in the world? Today children are hungry and dying of malnutrition. Why doesn't God do something to stop it? The world is full of loneliness, pain, suffering, abuse, and children crying and being hurt.

Erica paused where she was. Her heart was pounding, and there was a frustration in her voice as she read. She skipped over to the opposite page.

Why doesn't God do anything to stop it? There can only be a few possible reasons.

He is cruel.

He just doesn't care and is apathetic to us.

He isn't strong enough to do anything about it.

Or there just is no God.

Erica stopped reading. She looked up at Bishop North only to see a glimpse of his concerned face, so she quickly looked back down and shut her notebook. "That's why nothing you said the other night means anything to me. I'm sorry. I'll go open the front doors," Erica finally said in a different tone. After a long silence, she stood up.

"Please wait, Erica," Bishop North said. "I've always known there has been a lot of pain and hurt in your heart. I still don't know the extent of everything. But I don't think I've been a good friend if I've let you bottle up your feelings. I have not helped you see things in a better light, and I am so sorry," Bishop North said, catching her eyes for the first time. There she could see the pain he bore with her. "I know you might think that your arguments are watertight about God. But there are a lot of answers. May I share some of those with you?"

"I guess that is what we agreed to," Erica said, not entirely sure she wanted to hear anything different.

"I ask because I have met a few people over the years who I've talked to about God's goodness, and it becomes apparent they don't want to feel different. They have a vested interest in their feelings, and they want to be angry at God or dismiss Him," Bishop North said. "But I don't think you are one of those people, Erica."

"Maybe not," Erica said, almost under her breath.

"All scripture is great," Bishop North started as he opened his scriptures. "But there are a few passages that, in my opinion, are foundational. They are the verses that give us the tools to interpret all the other verses of scripture properly. Here's one of those. It is in 2 Nephi 26:24–25. Listen for the gold in this verse as I read it.

> He [God] doeth not anything save it be for the benefit of the world; for he loveth the world, even that he layeth down his own life that he may draw all men unto him. Wherefore, he

> commandeth none that they shall not partake of his salvation.
>
> Behold, doth he cry unto any, saying: Depart from me? Behold, I say unto you, Nay; but he saith: Come unto me all ye ends of the earth, buy milk and honey, without money and without price.

"Did you hear what's so special in that verse?" Bishop North asked.

"It claims that God is loving," Erica replied.

"It also makes two enormous claims with that. Not only that God is loving but also that He is actively trying to save every individual. It also says right at the beginning that God never does anything unless it will benefit the people of this world. Ever," Bishop North emphasized. "So now let's look at some of those events you mentioned under that lens. First, the Flood. How could the Flood have been a benefit to everyone involved?"

"You got me," Erica said, doubting that it could ever be viewed as a good thing.

"First of all, let's get a broader perspective," Bishop North said as he took out a blank piece of paper from the printer and began to draw.

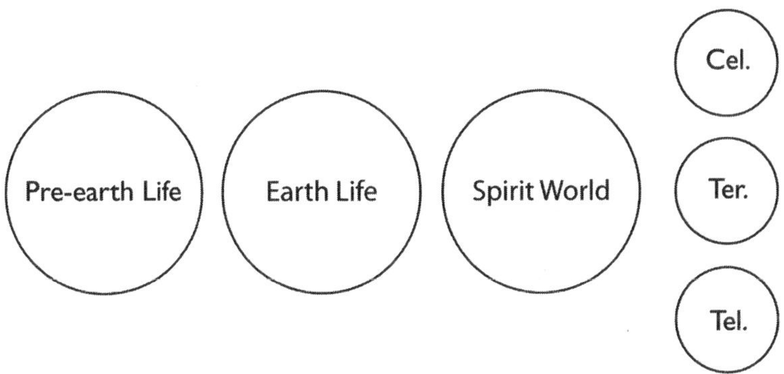

"Do you remember something called 'the plan of salvation' from when you were in Primary?" Bishop North asked as he showed Erica the rudimentary drawing.

"I don't remember much from back then," Erica replied. "It's been a long time."

"This chart of the plan of salvation is to express where we came from before we were born and what comes after this life. Before we were born," Bishop North pointed with his pen, "we lived with our Father in Heaven. He loved us more than any parent here has ever loved a child. And, like any good parent, He wanted us to grow, learn to be happy, and reach our fullest potential. We also loved Him and wanted to be like Him more than anything. But there were limits as to how much we could progress in that heavenly world. In order to progress and become like He was, we needed to experience the challenges that come from 'earth life.' In earth life, we would have more ability to make choices between good and evil. By choosing the good and rejecting the evil, we would progress and become more like our Heavenly Father. But God also knew that we would make mistakes, so He prepared a way for us to repent and make it back to Him. The premortal Jesus Christ offered Himself to suffer and die for us so that we could return to our Heavenly Father's presence. Knowing all the risks and challenges, we eagerly agreed to come down to earth. Many followed God and progressed, while many also chose evil. By Noah's time, most of the righteous people had been taken off of the earth, and the remainder of those left on the earth were almost entirely wicked. They had gotten to the point that every thought was about doing evil. The earth had become a sickening, sad, and violent place. Noah and his family had eventually become the only righteous people left on the earth."

"Okay," Erica jumped in. "I see how it was good for Noah and his family to be saved from the flood. They wouldn't have to deal with all those wicked people. But you said God didn't do anything except it benefited everyone," Erica objected. "How was it a benefit to the perhaps millions who drowned in the Flood?"

"Believe it or not, it was," Bishop North said. "This is where we need to look back at the chart. We need to remember that we lived prior to earth life and there is a lot after this life. Where does someone go when they die?" Bishop North asked, pointing to the chart.

"Spirit world," Erica said, looking down. "I'm not sure what that is."

"It is important to understand that all of the wicked who died in the flood didn't go straight to hell like much of the world believes. They went to the spirit world. God, in His mercy, removed them from their unredeemable, awful societies into the spirit world, where they would have the opportunity to be happy, to hear the gospel again, and to repent. It was the mercy of God that stopped them from sinning further and made it so they could still receive a kingdom of glory. We talked about grace before. Here is a perfect example of God and His goodness. Those wicked people on the earth had a chance to repent and rejected it. Still, in His mercy, God worked with them and helped them grow and progress to the degree they were willing to progress. It was not that they deserved more chances, it was because God is so gracious and good."

"It all seems a little too perfect," Erica said with some doubt in her voice.

"That's the exciting part," Bishop North said with a smile. "God's plan is perfect. It looks out for the welfare of each of His spirit children and helps all of them reach their fullest potential. There is also one more group of people we need to look at who were affected by the flood."

"Who?" Erica asked.

"Think of all of those who were yet to come to the earth and receive bodies," Bishop North challenged. "Imagine how, if you were Heavenly Father, you would want to send your precious spirit children to the best possible environments. If they were to be born into that completely wicked environment, they would have no chance for happiness, growth, and progress. It was also because of God's grace and goodness that he cleansed the earth so the future generations would have their chance to choose light over darkness."

"I'm still not convinced that killing someone can be kind," Erica said with a smirk.

"Erica, looking at the chart, what parts would I need to cut out to fit an atheist's beliefs?" Bishop North asked.

"Everything prior to earth life and everything after it," Erica said after studying the paper. "You would only leave earth life."

"That's right," Bishop North replied. "For an atheist, it would be like having blinders on, focusing them on this life because they think this is all there is. They believe when you die, you go into the great nothingness, where you would cease to exist. With that perspective, nothing could seem crueler than death. However, with the whole perspective God has given us, death is just a natural step we all take.

"Erica, try to imagine being back in heaven with your Heavenly Father. As you would look back over your pre-earth life, earth life, time in the spirit world, and being in the celestial kingdom, where would you identify as maybe being the low point of that journey?

"Low point?" Erica asked in clarification.

"You know, the period of time that was the most difficult."

"Maybe earth life," Erica sighed after some thought.

"Then why are we often most upset when someone moves on from this life?" Bishop North asked. "With the whole perspective of God's plan, moving on can be a great thing."

Erica wondered if it would be for her.

"One last thing about the Flood," Bishop North added, and he turned again in the scriptures. "How did God feel about destroying all these children of His who had become wicked? In the book of Moses we find God speaking with the prophet Enoch about all those who would be destroyed, and Enoch sees God weeping. Enoch wondered how God could weep. Seeing as how He has endless creations and He is so good, why would He weep about these wicked people being destroyed? God replies by saying that they are His creation and His children and He knows each one of them individually and perfectly. God goes on and says that He gave them their agency and commanded them to love each other, but they had gotten to the point that there was no affection left in them and they hated their own families. Touched by God's love and sorrow for these people, Enoch also wept for those people."

"What about killing children?" Erica asked. "Someone showed me once in the Bible where Moses' people were commanded to kill every man, woman, child, and every animal that breathed." Erica said. "I just can't see that as not being cruel."

"Did your friend also tell you why they were to be destroyed?" Bishop North asked.

"Wickedness," Erica said, making quotation marks with her fingers.

"Let me tell you of a few acts of wickedness that they were doing, and maybe you too will think God had the Israelites do the right thing," Bishop North said as he thumbed through his Old Testament. "In Leviticus eighteen the Lord said that the Israelites were not to live as the people of Canaan did or they would also be wiped out. Then He chronicled what those people were doing wrong. Here are just a few. God said that they were involved with every form of incest and sexual abuse in their families: adultery, sodomy, or homosexuality." He went on, "Also sexual relations with animals. After saying this, the Lord said, 'the land itself vomiteth out her inhabitants.' Can you see how it could have been in God's mercy for the children to be taken out of that hellish environment?"

"Yes," Erica said.

Bishop North waited, letting things process in Erica's mind. He was also praying inside, seeking inspiration and guidance for what to say or not.

"You didn't read everything you wrote there in your notebook," Bishop North said.

Erica stared down with a look of pain on her face and then shut the book. With an angry look in her eyes, she looked at her bishop.

"I'm sorry. I've pushed too far," Bishop North said as he moved to stand up.

"When I was growing up," Erica suddenly began to speak, "and when my mom was gone, my stepfather would . . ." Erica was breathing hard, with tears brimming up in her eyes. Bishop could see that she was squeezing her own arm in a way that looked painful, but he felt he couldn't say anything to stop her. Suddenly she broke down in sobs, unable to control herself. "He touched me and raped me," Erica finally said with a muffled voice, her head between her knees and her hands over her face.

If Erica had been able to look up, she would have seen that Bishop North was also weeping.

After minutes of crying together, Erica lifted her head up but didn't open her eyes. To her bishop she spoke. "Why did God let that happen to me? It went on for more than a year. I prayed constantly. Why didn't God prevent me from being hurt like that?"

Oh dear Father, why? Bishop North also cried out inside.

"So don't try to tell me about God's grace," Erica said with finality.

"Stay back here and rest," Bishop North said as he stood up and wiped his eyes. "I'll open up the doors and get things going. Rest here, Erica," he repeated.

"You don't need to worry about me," Erica said in the late afternoon as she locked the front doors to close. "It's been a long time now. My mom's former husband has been in jail for years," she went on in a cold, stoic voice. "It still hurts to think about, and I don't understand, but I'm okay. But now you understand why part of me wants to stay angry at God?"

"Maybe I can understand why," Bishop North said as he looked down at his hands. "Did I ever tell you about how I got this scar on my hand?" Erica looked down at the large pinkish scar on the backside of his right hand. She had seen it many times, but it had never seemed like the right time to ask about it. "I have also known abuse growing up. Like I said, I was taken away from my mother at an early age," Bishop North continued. "I can tell you about the scar another time, but I know what it is like to want to stay angry at God too. But I have also learned about the healing our Redeemer offers. The Lord has healed me, and He wants to do the same for you more than you can imagine.

"Now may not be the right time," Bishop North slowly went on to say. "But I want you to know that God wants to heal your pain. He can heal all the wounds from your life and make you whole again. He can even help you understand it all."

"You probably do have simple answers," Erica said. "But I really don't know if I want them."

"You also need to know this one thing," Bishop North went on. "As you have been hurting over the years, and as that terrible abuse was happening to you when you were younger, the Savior also felt all of your pain and suffered alongside you."

Erica just stared at Bishop North and then up at the ceiling. "How do you know that?" Erica finally inquired.

"Here is a scripture that expresses what we will realize when Jesus returns at His coming," Bishop North said as he turned in his scriptures. "In D&C 133 the Lord says:

> And now the year of my redeemed is come; and they shall mention the loving kindness of their Lord, and all that he has bestowed upon them according to his goodness, and according to his loving kindness, forever and ever.
>
> In all their afflictions he was afflicted. And the angel of his

> presence saved them; and in his love, and in his pity, he redeemed them, and bore them, and carried them all the days of old.

"So when Jesus comes, there is going to be an understanding of the Lord's 'loving kindness.' Then in verse 53 it says why we will feel that way. We will realize that in all our 'afflictions he was afflicted.' Erica," Bishop North went on, "Jesus knows our pains and sufferings because He has suffered all that we have suffered alongside us. Just like the flood, the Lord wept for His children and prepared a way to help them. The Lord is reaching out to you right now and has prepared a way to heal you."

"Simple," Erica said in a tone of disbelief. Her eyes were red as she looked up at the ceiling again.

"Actually it wasn't simple at all," Bishop North clarified. "It cost Jesus untold suffering to be able to know your pains and help you in this way. He paid the ultimate price for you because He loves you, Erica. No one has ever, or will ever, love you more.

"Something else that impresses me," Bishop North went on. "Is what is not going to be said when we see the Lord again. Over the years, I've met so many people that think they have a bone to pick with God. They think that they have a 'one up' on God and that things were not fair. They see their perceived argument against God as their excuse to choose evil. However, none of that will be mentioned because we will realize all that the Lord did for us. And like the verse said, although we didn't know it, the Lord's own presence saved us, and His love and pity redeemed us and carried us. There is nothing we suffer that the Lord did not unfairly suffer infinitely more, for our sakes. We will realize that 'surely he hath borne our griefs, and carried our sorrows.' "[1]

"So you're saying that Jesus has suffered everything that I and every person has suffered on this earth?" Erica asked. "Then why didn't He just stop it?"

"I'm not sure I understand what you mean," Bishop North said.

"If He was suffering too, why didn't He just stop what I was going through?" Erica asked in frustration. "He's all powerful, isn't He? He could have stopped my stepdad from doing any of the things he did. By doing that, Jesus could have saved Himself from suffering what I suffered, right?"

"I guess you're right," Bishop North confirmed after some thought. "He could have made it so much easier on Himself by just stopping all the suffering in the world. But I can think of two reasons that God generally doesn't do that."

"What?"

"The first reason, Erica, is agency," Bishop North said. "God made His children different than the animals, and He has given them the divine gift of choice. With animals, when they act a certain way, it is because of how they were created. We, on the other hand, have true choice. We are not wind-up robots that are destined and programmed to act in good or evil ways. Unlike the beasts, we actually have a choice to be good or bad. If God stopped every evil act and misstep, He would take all that agency and ability to choose away. It would take away our liberty."

"Maybe things would be better that way," Erica said.

"If God made some people to be good, and others to be bad, could we really congratulate the ones for being good and condemn the others for being bad?" Bishop North asked. "They were just doing what they were made to do. But God has made us to have real liberty in our choices. Yet if God took away all choices for evil, it would destroy our agency. Likewise, if God made us so that we would love Him, would it really be love? There has to be choice for it to really be love."

"So this world will have to be miserable," Erica stated in conclusion.

"I know it seems that way sometimes," Bishop North empathized. "I've felt the pains of this world too. But there is another reason for the opposition and pain of this earth life. Do you remember why we wanted to come to earth from the pre-earth life?"

"I think you said it was to become more like our Heavenly Father," Erica said. "But why did we have to leave our Heavenly Father to become more like Him? That doesn't make a lot of sense."

"There is something unique about this world that makes us stronger and more like Him," Bishop North said. "Resistance."

"What?" Erica asked to clarify.

"Erica, did you ever take a weight lifting class in high school?" Bishop North asked.

"Obviously not much," Erica said as she looked down at her

skinny arm. "But we did do a little weight lifting in a PE class."

"To build strong muscles," Bishop North went on to explain, "you need to be taken to your limit and a little beyond. For instance, let's say you were lying down and doing bench presses with a fifty-pound weight. Pretend you were easily able to do ten but now it is getting difficult. Do you remember what your spotter always told you?"

"One more!" Erica replied.

"So after you do another, then what?"

"One more!" Erica repeated.

"So let's say you go down again and give a Herculean effort but you can only get half way up and then you give out and the spotter catches the bar. Did you do good?"

"I think that is considered good when weight lifting," Erica stated with a puzzled look on her face.

"That's right," Bishop North confirmed. "In fact, did you know that the first ten easy lifts do almost no good to make you stronger? It's the last ones that really hurt and that last effort when you give out that will later build stronger muscles. What happens is that your muscles need to be taken to their limit, where they even begin to tear a bit from overexertion. Then when you are sore, your muscles tell your body that they need to be built stronger so that that level of exertion will not hurt them. So your body takes proteins to repair the microtears and builds your muscles back to be just a bit bigger and stronger. Then in the future, instead of ten lifts being easy, it may be twelve. And instead of maxing out at twelve, it might be fourteen or fifteen. And there are a lot of similarities between growing physically stronger and growing spiritually stronger."

"Does it always have to hurt?" Erica asked.

" 'No pain, no gain,' they say. This life is full of resistance and difficulties. Often we will be taken to the very limit of what we can handle, and even beyond. But if we keep trusting God and don't give up, He will make us into the godly men and women we decided in the pre-earth life we wanted to be."

"Let me show you one more of those foundational scriptures that help me understand this world," Bishop North said as he turned in his Bible. "With all the good and bad this world throws at us, the Apostle Paul made a bold declaration. He said, 'And we know that all things work together for good to them that love God, to them who are the called according to his purpose.' "

"I can believe that *many* difficult things in this life can help a person grow and become stronger," Erica said. "But I can't believe that *all* things can. Not the things I've been through. There is resistance, but other things just simply crush a person."

NOTE

1. Isaiah 53:4

chapter twelve

THE GOOD DEAL

"Come in," Joyce said with a smile as she greeted Anna and Caitlin with a hug. "You look so pretty, Anna. How are you two?"

Anna loved her older sister, Joyce, more than just about anyone else in the world. Anna admired the strength in Joyce and how she was humble enough to give honest compliments like she did. If you looked at any family picture of their family growing up, you would immediately point out Anna as the most beautiful in the family. Both had the same beautiful light red hair. Joyce, though, had a few more freckles and was a little on the plump side. Yet if you spent any time around the two sisters, it would quickly become evident that there was something in Joyce's smile that was magnetic and genuine. There were characteristics in Joyce that drew people to her. She really cared about people, though she might hardly know them. She also seemed wiser than most.

Joyce was one of those people who attracted friends. People liked to talk and share their problems with her because she understood others. This was partially because she'd had a generous helping of challenges in her life.[1] The sisters were also different in that Joyce was not as competitive as Anna. Whether it was a discussion or a game, it just didn't matter to Joyce if she won or not. For that reason, Anna always went to Joyce just to have a friend to talk with.

Anna likewise gave her sister a hug and sat down to talk about all Bishop North had discussed with her and what she had learned.

Then she shared how things were going with Mitch.

"What your bishop is saying sounds like just the right thing for you and Mitch," Joyce said after listening to her sister. "I like the term *grace*, though I never thought of it that way. Do you want to hear my take on it?"

"Sure," Anna said, always feeling like she stole too much of the conversation away from her sister.

"Maybe grace is simply giving more than what's expected. I learned a lesson like that when Burke and I were first married," Joyce said. Anna was never too thrilled with the man Joyce decided to marry. Anna felt that her sister deserved the most perfect guy in the world. Burke, on the other hand, was nice, but also goofy in appearance and social skills. "Nerd" was the word Anna might use to describe him. But despite Anna's mild and clandestine disapproval, Joyce and Burke were very happy together. "We had only been married about a year when some small things were starting to bother me. I would leave a little love note somewhere for him and then he would not write me one back. Soon I decided to write them less often. I looked around at other couples and figured they were not unthoughtful to each other like Burke had become. Then Burke did something that really hurt. I'm sure you noticed when you got married that your spouse has the power to hurt you more than anyone else."

"So true," Anna said sincerely but then waited for Joyce to continue.

"When I was hurting so badly, I decided in my bitterness that I would only be as nice to him as he was to me. When I saw he had stopped doing certain nice things for me, I would likewise stop doing nice things for him. Soon it became one of the most unhappy times in my life. It only lasted for about two months, but in that time our marriage went spiraling downward." Anna just listened, considering how her marriage was spiraling downward as they spoke, for similar reasons.

"Then I learned that the secret to happiness would be to give more than expected," Joyce said. "A little more kind, thoughtful, loving, and patient than one would naturally expect. I've found as I have done this, my life has been more rich and fulfilling."

"You definitely weren't a bad person before," Anna objected.

"You're kind," Joyce replied. "But after that I had more focus on how God wanted my life. Giving more than expected has given me more peace and satisfaction in life. Strangely, my life and marriage were pretty miserable when I just gave as I got."

"So did it change Burke at all?" Anna asked.

"I think it has quite a bit," Joyce said confidently with a smile.

"No offence, Joyce," Anna said, "but I think you're awesome, and from what I can see, you treat Burke much better than he treats you. He is getting the better deal than you."

"Well, I'm not sure you're right," Joyce said with a laugh. "But even if he were, would it matter? From what I gathered from what the bishop told you, justice is all about *getting* a good deal in relationships while grace is about *being* a good deal. I don't think the intent of grace is to manipulate someone else into treating you well. That would just be another form of justice. It's great if they do change, but I don't think it can be the whole intent."

"So you said Burke really hurt you. What did he do?" Anna asked sheepishly.

"I'm sorry, Anna," Joyce said. "You know I try not to talk bad about people. I think that applies even more when it has to do with your spouse."

"I was pretty sure you wouldn't tell," Anna said. "But, whatever he did, how did you get over it?"

Joyce replied, "One of my favorite quotes I've ever heard is, 'Holding a grudge is like drinking poison and hoping the other person dies.' " Anna laughed at how familiar the truth in that was. "So I just had to forgive him and let it go. Part of me wanted to stay mad and hold it over his head. Almost like it gave me power over him."

"I've done that too," Anna said. "Why would a person ever want to do that?"

"Maybe we think it helps justify all the mistakes we make," Joyce replied.

"Yeah, maybe," Anna said. "So if you're putting more into the relationship than the other, won't that just make you resentful every time you do something a little extra?"

"You really must not like Burke," Joyce said with a laugh. "He really isn't bad at all. In fact, he's a pretty great husband."

"Yeah, but you're awesome," Anna replied. "You deserve the best."

"I love you too, Anna," Joyce said, leaning over and giving Anna a hug. "Let me show you a scripture I learned in an institute class when I was in college." Joyce went in the bedroom of her apartment and brought back her scriptures. "It's where Paul is talking about charity. When Paul lists all the attributes of charity, he says:

> Charity suffereth long, and is kind; charity envieth not; charity vaunteth not itself, is not puffed up,
>
> Doth not behave itself unseemly, seeketh not her own, is not easily provoked, thinketh no evil;

"My teacher said that where the translation says, 'thinketh no evil,' the actual Greek word used was quite different. The word is the same as when one does bookkeeping. He said an alternative translation would be that charity 'doesn't keep a ledger.' "

"Charity doesn't keep score," Anna said, reiterating with a laugh.

"Not keeping score is a great piece of advice for a happy marriage," Joyce said with a smile.

"And I've kept count far too often," Anna said as her smile faded. Thinking over the past years, she remembered how when Mitch would do something particularly bad, she would make a mental note of it to remember for later. Almost as if she were collecting evidence to form a case against Mitch. But instead of a court of law, she was making a mental ledger of his wrongs so she could use those against him later in an argument. And she often would.

"Want to come with me to take Ashley to the playground?" Joyce offered as her daughter started to make some noise, waking from her nap. "Caitlin would love that," Anna said. The four started to walk to the play area in the middle of the six buildings at the apartment complex.

"I told the bishop that it's hard to show goodness to someone when you don't feel that love for them," Anna said as Ashley and Caitlin ran off to the slide.

"You don't feel anything for him?" Joyce questioned.

"Not much," Anna said as they sat on a bench facing the play area.

"You're bringing up another memory from institute class that semester," Joyce said. "I remember also learning that in English there is essentially one word for love while in Greek there are four words."

"What are they?" Anna wondered aloud.

"I can't remember all the Greek words, but one of them was for romantic love, one was for love like between family members, one was for love like between friends, and one was what we often call charity. When Burke and I got married, I started to see all four of those loves balancing between us. At first romantic love was huge. I remember that when dating, I thought that if there was only this one aspect of love, we could live happily on just that alone. But quickly after getting married, I found how necessary it was to also have the strong friendship love. Unless we could talk, romantic love just wouldn't be enough. I also grew to love him as family, which made our bond stronger still. Lastly, I needed that charity for when things went wrong. It's like these four types are pieces of a pie, taking different sizes of importance at certain times. So which types of love are most crucial to your marriage right now?"

"I would guess charity and family love would be the most important right now, in order to get through this," Anna said as she watched Caitlin and Ashley play. "Mitch is my husband, and we have a family that I don't want to tear apart."

"In some ways, Mitch isn't really the problem," Anna continued. "It's me."

"What do you mean?" Joyce asked.

"Some people bring out the best in a person; others bring out the worst. I wonder if Mitch and I are like that for each other. Perhaps the problem is I don't like who I've become with him. We just aren't good for each other." As Anna was speaking, she noticed a young couple walking together with a stroller. The man was pushing, the young woman had her arm in his, and they were laughing about something. As Anna looked discreetly at them, she couldn't help but feel stinging jealousy.

"Any chance that somewhere in Mitch is the man of your dreams?" Joyce asked, looking away from the couple and capturing Anna's attention back.

"I really don't know," Anna replied. "The other day I was looking in the classifieds for a garage sale. By chance I looked over at the personals. There I read of a man who was looking for someone to go for walks and hikes with. It says he was looking for someone who didn't want to waste their life in front of a TV. I thought to myself, 'I want that.' "

"But Anna," Joyce started, trying to carefully choose her words, "I've never known you to hike much. And you spend a fair amount of time with the TV, don't you?"

"Yeah," Anna laughed. "But I still want something different. I want to start fresh and be with a person who makes me want to be that kind of person in the personals."

"Remember when we were in Young Women together," Joyce started in a seemingly different direction, "and they would have us write down the characteristics we wanted in a spouse?"

Anna laughed as she nodded. It was an activity the Young Women leaders seemed to do some variation on at least twice a year.

"Then do you remember how it would usually conclude?" Joyce asked.

"If you want to marry that kind of person, you have to *be* that kind of person first,"[2] Anna replied. "I guess I should have stuck to my list," she added.

"But you're missing the point, Anna," Joyce said in the kind way that only she could. "It's no different now that you're married. You still have to try to be that spouse you wish Mitch would be."

"To try to change him?" Anna objected.

"No," Joyce lovingly replied. "Do it because you want to be that person and God wants you to be that person." As Joyce spoke, the young couple turned the corner behind an apartment building.

"You're right," Anna replied in a discouraged tone. "Don't get mad at me, but I can't help but think that all of it would be easier with a different guy. Here, maybe this expresses how I feel," Anna said as she shuffled through her purse and pulled out her MP3 player. After finding the song she wanted, Shenandoah's "I Want to Be Loved Like That," she listened for a bit and then handed Joyce the headphones. The music played, and Joyce listened to the lyrics about timeless love.

"Is it so wrong that 'I want to be loved like that'?" Anna said, repeating the words from the song.

"We all want to be loved like that," Joyce replied. "I think it is a universal desire to want to be loved with the kind of unselfish, perfect love that's expressed in the song. That is the compelling kind of love that the Lord has for us, which draws us to Him—'grace,' as your bishop put it."

"And shouldn't that love also be in our marriage?" Anna asked to make a point.

"Absolutely, but there is a mistake the song makes," Joyce replied after pausing to think. "Sure we want people to love us like that. But are we only willing to love others like that if they first love us with that kind of love? With the gospel of Jesus Christ, Jesus wants us to be the one to love like that first. He wants us to be the initiator. Jesus wants us to be the one to start it and infuse that kind of gracious love into all our relationships."

"So the Lord wants me to start loving Mitch with that gracious love," Anna said as they both looked off at the kids playing.

"Actually," Joyce began again, "what I said about Jesus wanting us to be the initiator isn't exactly true. The Savior has been the initiator. Jesus started it. He has shown that love to us so that now we can go start that love in the relationships around us. He didn't wait for us to first love Him. He started loving us first."

"Okay," Anna said with strengthened resolve. "I'm going to do it. I really am going to give it all I can. I have nothing to lose and, like you pointed out, whether he changes or not, it will change me more into the person I want to be. Either way, I want to learn to love like that."

Joyce leaned over and gave her sister a hug and then the two watched Ashley and Caitlin playing with the other kids that had come.

"There's one last thing that I haven't told you yet. It makes me sure that I can't keep things the way they are," Anna added. "I'm pregnant."

NOTES

1. Those who know life's difficulties are better able to minister to others who are in the midst of trials. In 2 Corinthians 1:4 we read of the Savior, "Who comforteth us in all our tribulation, that we may be able to comfort them which are in any trouble, by the comfort wherewith we ourselves are comforted of God."

2. To attract the right person, we have to be the right person. Perhaps the scriptural basis for this teaching is in Doctrine and Covenants 88:40, "For intelligence cleaveth unto intelligence; wisdom receiveth wisdom; truth embraceth truth; virtue loveth virtue; light cleaveth unto light; mercy hath compassion on mercy and claimeth her own; justice continueth its course and claimeth its own; judgment goeth before the face of him who sitteth upon the throne and governeth and executeth all things."

chapter thirteen

THE WORST OF BOTH WORLDS

"Do you feel any better about things?" Bishop North asked Erica as the two of them sat down on the curb and looked up to face a beautiful sunset. The sun had just crossed over the mountains in the west, and now orange-colored clouds were beginning to turn to shades of red. To a passerby, the two looked like employees taking a break, although the store was now closed.

"I do and I don't," Erica replied. "I see what you believe about how God isn't cruel. But I don't know if I believe it all. I guess that comes from being angry at God for a long time. And I'm not good at change."

"But it's kind of funny," Bishop North said as he looked at the colors in the sky. "The God who has given us so much beauty and blesses us so much; the One who has sent prophets to guide us away from the dangers of this world and has given us our agency; the One whose whole purpose is to bless and help us—He becomes the great scapegoat. The One who has tried to do the most for us gets blamed for all of the bad in the world.

"And then consider how ironic it is with Satan," Bishop North continued. "A being whose whole purpose is to cause pain, suffering, and sorrow. Although his whole drive is to cause chaos and misery, I don't think I've ever seen a person shake an angry fist down at Satan."

Erica gave a subtle laugh as she imagined someone yelling at Satan with their face toward the ground. "I guess the devil does get off pretty easy," Erica concluded.

"And God gets all the blame," Bishop North added again.

"I think there is a lot you know about God that I just don't," Erica said.

"What do you mean?"

"You just seem to have this connection with God, and I hardly know who He is," Erica replied.

"You know, Erica, there's something really neat about that," Bishop North said. "Often with those we admire, the more we learn about them and the closer we come to them, the less extraordinary they become in our eyes. But the great exception to that rule is our Lord Jesus Christ. The Savior becomes all the more amazing at close examination."

"Okay then, who is He?" Erica challenged with a small smile.

Bishop North knew that these feelings Erica was now expressing were rare for her. She wasn't one to want to talk about these kinds of things, but the current circumstances and the Lord's Spirit had opened her heart. Bishop North drew in a big breath as he looked again at the sunset. Inside he prayed for the Lord's inspiration and to be an instrument in God's hand to further touch Erica's heart. "Okay, maybe the first point to make is that we come to know God the Father through His Son, Jesus Christ. Since the Fall of Adam and Eve, one of the biggest missions of the Savior is to teach us about God the Father. There is no virtue or character trait that one has and the other doesn't. They are one. So by coming to know the Savior, we are inherently coming to know the Father."

"Okay, but why is that so important?" Erica asked.

"Because as we talk about God, we'll have to get most of our examples and illustrations by looking at His Son, the Lord Jesus Christ," Bishop North said. "It is not possible to know and grow in love for one without growing in love for the other. They are not one in body, but like I said, the Savior is so perfectly in line with the Father's will that coming to know the Savior is coming to know the Father. So when we talk about God's goodness, we will generally look to examples of Jesus Christ as the Lord of the Old Testament and the Lord of all scripture."

"Fair enough," Erica said. "What's the next point about God?"

"Well, let's go in a separate direction for a minute," Bishop

North said. "Of all of the billions of people who have lived on this earth, who do you think has suffered the worst physical pain?"

"I don't know," Erica started as she considered the question. "I've heard about the awful ways captured soldiers have been tortured in wars. It makes me sick to think that one human could do those kinds of things to another. Maybe one of those tortured soldiers has suffered the worst physical pain."

"Next question," Bishop North went on. "How about tragedy. Who do you think has suffered the worst tragedies in life?"

"Maybe one of those pioneers who lost their family to sickness while crossing the plains," Erica replied after some thought. "Losing your whole family has to rank high on the tragedy scale."

"I agree," Bishop North replied. "Next, what individual do you think has suffered the greatest feelings of dark depression?"

"I don't know. Maybe someone who finally gave in to the hidden darkness and killed himself," Erica said, starting to feel frustrated with the questions. "What are you getting at with all these questions?"

"It's this," Bishop North said. "Without a doubt, the answer to all of those questions, of who has suffered the worst, is our Lord, Jesus Christ."

"How?" Erica questioned.

"In the garden of Gethsemane, and on the cross, Jesus suffered the fulness of every person's sufferings in life. He completely suffered every torture ever given. He suffered every man and woman's depression in its intensity and entirety. He felt every tragedy and loss. No matter the example of suffering we may come up with, Jesus felt that person's sufferings along with the sufferings of every other person who has ever lived or ever would live. For this reason, no person even comes close to having suffered as much as the Savior. He felt every loneliness, shame, hate, and regret. He suffered every hurt, including your pains and mine."

Erica sat there as she considered the idea. She found it hard to believe that someone would take pain like that upon himself. "But in your original question, you asked about what *person* had suffered the most. Jesus isn't really a person like you and me."

"Then there's the next question. Is Jesus Christ god or man?" Bishop asked.

"Well, we don't believe He is the same individual as God the

Father, right?" Erica asked.

"Right," Bishop North confirmed. "But does that mean that Jesus was just a man?"

"That doesn't seem right, either," Erica said with a confused expression.

"So is Jesus god or man?" Bishop North asked again.

Erica let the question hang in the air, showing by her expression that she did not know.

"The answer is *yes*," Bishop North finally said. "Jesus is both fully god and fully man. He is god in that He is a member of the godhead and has the divine power of being a god.[1] He was also a man by being born of a mortal mother. Perhaps that is why Jesus was called the 'Son of God' and 'Son of Man.' "

"I've never thought of Jesus as a person before," Erica said. "Not like you and me. In some ways it is a lot easier to see Him as nothing like us."

"Yet He was fully human like you and me," Bishop North interjected, "except without any sin."

"Thinking of Jesus as divine and a god seems to make sense," Erica said. "But why did He have to be a man also?"

"Let me answer by asking another question," Bishop North replied. "What is the difference between empathy and sympathy?"

"I think," Erica started, "with sympathy you just feel bad for someone, but with empathy, you feel bad because you know how they feel. You've been there before."

"So which does the Savior have for us: empathy or sympathy?"

"I'm not sure," Erica replied.

"The Savior's life was lived so that He would understand and know us," Bishop North replied. "If Jesus was completely different from us and never left His heavenly home, how could He understand our pains and sorrows? That's why he had to become human like us. He had to become one of us."

"I don't think I understand," Erica said.

"Do you know what it feels like to be a bird?" Bishop North questioned. "We might be able to imagine, but we could never know unless we were to become one. Likewise, the Savior had to become fully human to understand human pains and sorrows."

"So Jesus had to become human so He could suffer like us?" Erica tried to clarify.

"Yes, that's part of it." Bishop North said. "And Jesus didn't have an easy life either. He was born into poverty, on the run; owned almost nothing; was unfairly persecuted; and was put to death between two thieves. He knew hunger, pain, and sorrow just like you and me."

"But there are some things He couldn't know," Erica said. "Like childbirth. Or the types of things I've been through."

"Remember that scripture we talked about before that said, 'In all their afflictions he was afflicted'? Jesus knows even those things. In the hours of Gethsemane and on the cross, Jesus came to know the pains and sorrows of every person throughout time. I don't understand how He did it, but I know He did it. The Lord loved you and me so much that He experienced every pain we would ever bear. That is why He has true empathy. He has actually suffered our pains right alongside us. When you are tempted to think that no one knows how you feel, He can gently raise His hand and say, 'I do. I know how you feel—perfectly.' No sorrow or pain of ours escaped Him."

Erica thought about the Savior's sufferings for her as she looked at the sky's colors, which were turning from reds to darker purples and grays. "But don't forget He was a god also," Erica interrupted the silence. "Surely that had to make things a bit easier for Him. Being god and man."

"I can see how one could think that," Bishop North said. "But actually the opposite is true. In reality, being God in the flesh made things harder for Him. Jesus had the worst of both worlds. The worst of being man and the worst of being God."

"The worst of being a human makes sense," Erica said. "But is there a downside to being a god?"

"There are actually quite a few," Bishop North replied. "But here is one point to consider. The purpose of Jesus's life was such that none of us will ever be able to say, 'But He had it easier.' His life was in all ways more difficult than any life ever lived. He faced every difficulty, temptation, and suffering that a person can face in this life. If His life were to be easier than others, then He couldn't truly be a reasonable, valid example for us. Yet He lived perfectly in the same world we stagger and fall in every day."

"Okay then, what are the downsides of being a god?" Erica said in a doubting voice.

"Have you ever heard the saying, 'Power corrupts, and absolute power corrupts absolutely'?"

"I might have," Erica replied.

"That has proven so true with those with power on this earth. But the great exception to this is in the case of the one being that truly had absolute power: the Lord Jesus Christ. Being God in the flesh, there could have been intense temptations for self-gratification to make life easier. When Satan first came to tempt Jesus, Satan wanted Jesus to turn a stone to bread. Although Jesus had been fasting a long time, Jesus was not to use His powers for self-indulgence. Likewise, Satan tempted Him to prove Himself by casting Himself off a building and then miraculously saving Himself. Jesus could have done it, but again, Jesus knew He wasn't to use His power to prove Himself or perform stunts. Also imagine what He could have done when He was being persecuted. Erica, have you ever been intentionally spit on?"

Erica thought back to the sixth grade when some freshmen girls were picking on her. They were taunting her to fight even though they were much bigger. "Just once," she replied.

"How did you feel about it?" Bishop asked, prying deeper.

"I've rarely felt more anger," Erica replied after a pause. "It started a fight, and I was suspended for a week."

"Jesus was spit on too," Bishop North said. "Beat, spit on, and scourged. In situations like that, there would only be so much we could do. But with Jesus, imagine the discipline of restraining the power He had. With the ease of a blink, He could have expired each of His persecutors' lives. And then imagine how all that power would be even worse during the hours of the Atonement."

"What do you mean?" Erica questioned.

"Hold your hand out like you're going to receive something."

Erica did so with a puzzled look on her face.

"Imagine I just took a live coal from a fire, and in order to save the lives of everyone you have ever cared about, you will have to let me place the burning coal in your hand and you will need to hold it until it is cool. Do you think you could do it?"

"I don't know," Erica said as she thought about the excruciating pain that comes with burning. "It would be hard to fight the reflex of just jerking my hand away."

"Could you do it?" Bishop asked again.

"I think I would try."

"Then one more thing," Bishop North said. "You have a choice. You can choose to have your hand strapped down to a table, or you could simply hold it there by your self will. Which would you choose?"

"I would want it strapped down," Erica answered.

"Why?"

"I would fear that my own determination wouldn't be enough."

"But you see, Erica," Bishop North now said slowly. "Jesus could never be held down. The pain of burning we imagined would only be the smallest drop in the ocean of suffering that Jesus experienced. During the hours of the Atonement as each feeling of suffering and pain and sin came crashing upon Him, He could have made it stop. It would have been frighteningly easy for Jesus to make it stop as every particle of His body and soul screamed for deliverance. He was God in the flesh. He had the complete ability to make it all stop at His will. Yet He remained in that garden as He suffered. Erica, were the nails really what held Jesus to the cross?"

"No," Erica said as her eyes narrowed upon a twig in her hands. "I guess not."

"Then what held the Savior there?"

There was something in Erica that didn't want to answer. This was the first time she had considered God to be a being of such love. "His love, I suppose," Erica finally answered.

"His personal love for you, Erica," Bishop North added, "and for me. That's what held our Lord there in His sufferings. If Jesus didn't continue on, it would have left you and I lost in death and hell forever."

"So if being a god didn't make it easier, then why did He have to be a god at all?"

"A friend of mine once explained it to me this way," Bishop North replied. 'From Mary He could suffer. From God He could suffer infinitely.' "[2]

"What does that mean?" Erica asked.

"Imagine a person is in a horrible accident and in extreme pain. What will often happen to a person while in that kind of tremendous pain?"

"They black out or maybe go into a coma," Erica replied.

"Yes," Bishop North said. "In mercy, God made our bodies such that when pain becomes too unbearable, our bodies will naturally lose consciousness. Because of our mortality, had we started to feel the crushing weight of what Jesus experienced in the garden and on the cross, each of us would have been crushed into nothingness. But because Jesus was also a god, He did not have to submit to unconsciousness like we would. Being a man, He felt everything like we would, but being a god, He was able to suffer infinite amounts of pain without His ability to remain conscious being taken away from Him."

"You're right," Erica said. "That doesn't sound like such a great aspect of being a god."

"So there you have it. The worst of both worlds," Bishop North said. "The worst of being man, in that Jesus could suffer and hurt just like we do. And the worst of being a god because He could feel that hurt in infinite amounts, without surrendering to death." Bishop North stood up from the curb and stretched. "So there's a look at who Jesus was, but still we have hardly touched on what it was He suffered for you and me. Go home, Erica. Tomorrow we will look at the heart of it all. We will look deeper into the Atonement."

Erica thought about her life and God as she walked home. As she reached for the doorknob of her apartment, the door swung open, and Erica jumped out of the way as her roommate ran past. "Steve's inside," her roommate said as she briefly turned around on her way down the sidewalk. "He's been waiting an hour for you to get home. Have fun."

Erica looked down at the shadows revealed from the cracked open door in front of her. After some thought, she went inside.

NOTES

1. As Church members, we often don't like to refer to Jesus as God because we know that Jesus is not the same being as God the Father. Yet he still bears the title of being God. Bruce R. McConkie stated, "Such is the plain and pure pronouncement of all the prophets of all the ages. In our desire to avoid the false and absurd conclusions contained in the creeds of Christendom, we are wont to shy away from this pure and unadorned verity; we go to great lengths to use

language that shows there is both a Father and a Son, that they are separate Persons and are not somehow mystically intertwined as an essence or spirit that is everywhere present. Such an approach is perhaps essential in reasoning with the Gentiles of sectarianism; it helps to overthrow the fallacies formulated in their creeds.

"But having so done, if we are to envision our Lord's true status and glory, we must come back to the pronouncement of pronouncements, the doctrine of doctrines, the message of messages, which is that Christ is God. And if it were not so, he could not save us" (Bruce R. McConkie, *The Promised Messiah* [Salt Lake City: Deseret Book, 1978], 98). Other scriptures that make this very clear are Mosiah 15:13; 3 Nephi 11:14; and D&C 19:16, 18.

2. I first heard this thought from Mark Eastmond in his Book of Mormon Conference 2001 presentation.

chapter fourteen

CHANGE

Dear Bishop,

I'm sure you cringe every time you see an email from me. But don't worry. I'm not writing to argue. I've decided that you and the Lord are right. I'm going to show Mitch grace like the Lord wants me to. I'm fully committed (aren't you happy now?)!

But the problem is I'm not sure what exactly to do. I know that grace is showing goodness to the others beyond or without regard for what they have done or what they deserve, but what exactly do I do? Any suggestions?

Anna

As Bishop North read the email, he felt an urge to write down a bunch of ideas, but then he fought it.

Dear Anna,

I'm so happy for your decision. I'm so grateful for what you are allowing the Lord to do in your life and what He will do in your marriage and family by your decision.

I was about to write you a list of suggestions but then I felt that would rob you of the experience. You need to ponder and pray on this. Let the Lord guide you on how He would have you show His goodness to Mitch.

But here are some things to ponder as you think about how to show grace. Remember that grace is in your *words* and in your *actions*. It is in what you say and what you choose not to say. It is in what you do and choose not to do.

Also, please expect resistance. You can anticipate that Mitch will probably not react the way you want him to at first. Have you ever push-started a car before? At first it is really hard, but once you get it moving and establish some momentum by your persistence, it isn't so hard to keep it going. Change in marriage is the same way. Expect it to be very hard at first, but I promise it will get easier with persistence and your commitment. For this reason you need to decide what you will do to continue your commitment to the Lord when Mitch doesn't respond like you might expect.

I'll be praying for you and Mitch.

Bishop

He isn't going to make this easy, Anna thought as she finished reading the email. She pulled out a notepad and said a prayer. *Father, I want a good marriage. Please forgive me for all the many mistakes I've made. Please help me in my commitment to show grace. Help me to love Mitch more and be able to show him greater love. Help me to know the things I should do and the ways you want me to show grace to Mitch. . .*

As Anna finished her prayer, she thought how Bishop North had said that grace was in words and actions. *Let's start with words*, she thought, and she wrote down ideas.

Identify 5 things he does well and compliment him.
Go for a whole day without criticizing anything he does.
Ask for forgiveness for my faults toward him.
Take the trouble to make a meal he especially likes.
Write a kind note.
Pray for him.
Don't keep score on what he does versus what I do.
Give him a flower.
Go on a creative date with some effort behind it.
Tell him something I admire about him.

As Anna continued to write she occasionally got discouraging thoughts like, *Why doesn't he ever do these things for me?* But each time she remembered that it wasn't about him as much as it was about her and how she needed—and wanted—to be a better person. The Golden Rule she had been taught in primary popped into her head: "Do unto others as you would have others do unto you."

After writing the list, Anna sat down on the couch and thought about how things could become difficult once Mitch came home from work. Then she thought about what Bishop North had said about expecting resistance and push-starting a car. She wondered if she would have strength to be the person she should be when Mitch had a knack for getting her upset.

Anna thought about all these things as she opened her scriptures. By chance she turned the page and noticed a verse highlighted that she couldn't recall ever marking: Doctrine and Covenants 38:24.

> And let every man esteem his brother as himself, and practise virtue and holiness before me.

They have practice *spelled wrong*, she thought. *And how do you practice virtue anyway?* Then Anna's mind went back to the other night when she blew up at Mitch. After he had left the room, and Anna was steaming, she thought about what she would say if Mitch came back and started to get upset with her. She had rehearsed and played out in her mind different possibilities of what she might say and do depending on what he might say. She came up with a lot of good comebacks to his rudeness. Most of the thoughts were how she would tear him apart with her words, if the situation presented itself. She had *practiced* it all out in her mind.

Then she thought of her concern that she would not be able to act with the graciousness she planned. *Maybe I've been practicing the wrong way*, she thought. *In my mind, I've been practicing out vice instead of virtue.* Then Anna started to reflect on common situations where Mitch got her mad. For each of those situations, she decided how she would act instead of react. It was like she needed to have an alternative course to take rather than the common reactions she had normally taken with Mitch.

"Hey Mitch," Anna said with a mini smile as her husband came home from work.

"Hi," he replied with a slightly confused look on his face. "I thought you were still mad at me."

"I was," Anna said. "But I'm not anymore. I was a little quick to get angry the other day."

"Okay," Mitch said, feeling more confused. He could feel something in the air that made him uneasy. He knew something was different but wasn't sure how to react. "Is everything all right?"

"I'm not sure. But I want it to be," Anna said. "What I mean is, I've been less than the kind of person I've wanted to be with you. I want to change."

"By that, are you really saying you want me to change?" Mitch interrupted.

"No," Anna said. At first she felt anger start inside her. But then she considered how it could have sounded to him. She let out a small laugh. "I'm serious in that I want to be a better person than I've been here at home. I want to be a better person to you than I've been. That's all."

Mitch looked at Anna with no expression and then turned and started to walk up the stairs. "We'll see how long this lasts," Mitch said just loud enough for Anna to hear. Anger surged up in Anna. She thought how he was the one who should be apologizing and changing. But Anna quickly caught herself. "Mitch," she said as he neared the top of the stairs. "I want it to last. But I need your help. Change is hard for me. But I really want to change. I want our relationship to be better too. Can you help me?"

Mitch looked back, feeling stunned. He knew his wife, and this was not at all how he expected her to react. He was sure Anna was going to blow up at him, and for those moments he felt a strange satisfaction in knowing she would. But when she didn't blow, he was shocked. "Sure," Mitch said, feeling out of his comfort zone again.

As Mitch got in his car the next morning, he saw a sticky note on a writable CD propped up on the steering wheel.

Dear Mitch,

Sorry I was up so late last night. I was thinking back to how we used to be together. How I would like it to be again. It brought back so many thoughts and got me going with burning this CD. I hope you also enjoy the memories.

Love,
Your wife

He held up the CD. There was a part of him that didn't want to put it in. He wasn't sure why, but part of him was angry at what Anna was doing. Yet curiosity won him over so that halfway to work, he put in the CD. What he heard were ten of the songs from the time period Anna and he had been dating, engaged, and newly married. *I love how things were back then*, he thought.

chapter fifteen

THE CUP

"Good morning," Bishop North said as Erica entered the bakery early to find her boss far along in the work. As Erica took off her jacket, a fine golden chain bearing a small cross fell against her tank top.

"How are you?" Bishop North asked as he turned to face Erica and spontaneously gave out a small laugh when he saw the little cross. Quickly he suppressed his amusement with a smile and turned back around.

"What?" Erica asked. "You don't like it?"

"Oh, it's fine," Bishop North replied. "Maybe our talk yesterday was more successful than I thought."

"Or maybe I thought it might be something to make you mad at me," Erica said.

"If you tried harder, I'm sure you could figure out something to get me upset." Bishop North smiled. "But it wouldn't stop me from caring about you. I think of you like a daughter."

"Should I take it off?" Erica tried as she held it up. "It doesn't offend you, does it?"

"Not a bit," Bishop North replied. "Keep it on. Maybe I should be glad you found religion."

"I don't think I have," Erica said honestly, sighing as she thought about her old boyfriend being over the night before. "I've thought a lot about our discussion and my life, but I honestly think I'm more confused than ever. Maybe that church down the street can help."

"Yeah, maybe," Bishop North replied with a smile. "But maybe we are going about this the wrong way."

"What do you mean?"

"Let's get a few loaves in and then we'll talk about that cross around your neck."

After a late night with Steve, Erica had decided she didn't want to talk to her boss anymore about religion. But there in the bakery, she had a hard time resisting more discussion. She felt sure her life wouldn't change much, but there was a strong desire in her to at least understand more.

"Okay, so you don't like my cross, after all," Erica said as they put the last loaves in to bake.

"I love it," Bishop replied. "It is a symbol that is sacred to millions around the world. But I think it might not be the right symbol to have around your neck."

"What? Is CTR better?"

"No," Bishop said, smiling. "But that cross might not give the message you want it to give. *Atonement* is the word we use when talking about the Savior's suffering and death for us. Jesus often taught using symbols. Erica, do you know what symbol the Lord used when referring to the suffering He would feel in the Garden of Gethsemane and on the cross?"

"Not a cross?" Erica tried.

"No," Bishop North replied. "He talked about the symbol of the cross as what His disciples should take up, but He never referred to His Atonement with that word."

"Then what symbol did He use?"

"Father," Bishop began to quote, "if it be possible, let this cup pass from me: nevertheless not as I will, but as thou wilt."

"A cup?" Erica questioned.

"A small golden cup might look a little different hanging from that necklace around your neck," Bishop North gestured. "But it's the symbol Jesus consistently used to refer to His Atonement."[1]

"Why a cup?"

"In these verses in Doctrine and Covenants 19, I'll show you," Bishop North said as he turned in his scriptures. "Here the Lord is telling an individual how desperately he needs to repent. While I read this, try to figure out more about this cup."

> Therefore I command you to repent—repent, lest I smite you by the rod of my mouth, and by my wrath, and by my anger, and your sufferings be sore—how sore you know not, how exquisite you know not, yea, how hard to bear you know not.
>
> For behold, I, God, have suffered these things for all, that they might not suffer if they would repent;
>
> But if they would not repent they must suffer even as I;
>
> Which suffering caused myself, even God, the greatest of all, to tremble because of pain, and to bleed at every pore, and to suffer both body and spirit—and would that I might not drink the bitter cup, and shrink—
>
> Nevertheless, glory be to the Father, and I partook and finished my preparations unto the children of men.

"What's in the cup?" Bishop asked.

"Suffering, I guess,"

"Suffering for all the pains, sorrows, and sins this world would ever produce," Bishop North added. "What is the taste of the contents of that cup?"

Erica looked over the verses again. "Bitter."

"Bitter from what?" Bishop prodded on.

"I suppose it's bitter from all the evil. Bitter from our awful sins."

"That's right," Bishop said. "Jesus never committed a sin. He was pure and had never known the bitterness of sin like you and I. Yet there in Gethsemane and on the cross, He partook of this metaphorical cup and suffered all the evils of this world. And just like you, Erica, He did not deserve what He suffered because of any sin of His own."

"I'm not sure I understand what it means to suffer for sin," Erica said.

"If you're like me, I'm sure you have made mistakes," Bishop North said. "How did it feel afterwards? What are some words you would use to describe the feelings that come from sin?"

"Regret, darkness," Erica started as she thought back over mistakes she had made. "Fear, loneliness, self-loathing. I've felt lower than pond scum. Sometimes I felt like I wanted to crawl into a hole and die."

"And all of that, and more, is what Jesus took upon himself," Bishop North said as he opened his scriptures. "In Alma thirty-six, we get a glimpse of what suffering for just our own sins would be like. Alma the Younger was a very wicked man during the first part of his life. God sent an angel, who told him to repent. Alma went into a comalike condition for three days in which he felt the pains of a damned soul. Then in verse 12, Alma begins to tell how he felt as he suffered for his sins. He said:

> But I was racked with eternal torment, for my soul was harrowed up to the greatest degree and racked with all my sins.
>
> Yea, I did remember all my sins and iniquities, for which I was tormented with the pains of hell; yea, I saw that I had rebelled against my God, and that I had not kept his holy commandments.
>
> Yea, and I had murdered many of his children, or rather led them away unto destruction; yea, and in fine so great had been my iniquities, that the very thought of coming into the presence of my God did rack my soul with inexpressible horror.
>
> Oh, thought I, that I could be banished and become extinct both soul and body, that I might not be brought to stand in the presence of my God, to be judged of my deeds.

"In that first verse it talks about being 'racked' and 'harrowed up.' Do you know what he means by those words?"

Erica shook her head no.

"A harrow is a farming device. Usually it has large, heavy spikes, and it's pulled behind a tractor or animal, which would tear and pull up the ground to make it ready for planting. A rack was a torture device used to stretch and pull a person apart. Here Alma is saying that he felt his soul was being plowed up and ripped apart from the inside. Alma was feeling what it was like to suffer for his own sins. But Jesus took the cumulative weight of Alma's sins and added that with all the sins of all people who have or ever will live."

"So my sins were combined with everyone else's?" Erica asked.

"I'm not sure I know what you mean," Bishop said, feeling there was more in what she was asking.

Erica looked over at a work table and grabbed a four-cup, tempered glass measuring cup. She didn't hold it by the handle but held the large cup carefully with her fingertips beneath. "Were my sins mixed in with everyone else's?" Erica asked as she casually pretended to swirl an invisible mixture with her finger.

"Erica," Bishop North began to say after considering her question. "When Christ was suffering the infinite weight of the Atonement, were we anonymous to Him? As He partook of the cup, could the Lord distinguish for *what* and for *whom* He was actually suffering? Was there a name to His pains, or were you and I and our individual contributions unknown to Him? Were our individual contributions somehow mixed up in the cup beyond the Savior's ability to identify?"

"Yeah," Erica said. "I guess that is what I'm asking. Was it simply a blinding load of suffering placed on Jesus?"

"Or more personal?" Bishop North asked, completing her thought. "What do you think? Which way would you hope it was?"

"Something in me hopes it was not personal," Erica said. A grave look covered her face, and she looked out the window.

"I think I know what you mean," Bishop North said. "We like to be anonymous when we've done something wrong. It's kind of terrifying to think that the Lord could have known it was me as He suffered and bled for me. But that is the question now, isn't it?" Bishop North asked as he stood up and looked in the drawer of his office desk. "Years ago, I started to wonder that same thing. I searched for an answer to this question and found a few things." Bishop North pulled out a couple of folded papers. "Listen to these statements while considering how personal the Atonement was.

"Merrill J. Bateman of the First Quorum of the Seventy spoke about this when he said:

> The Savior, as a member of the Godhead, knows each of us personally. Isaiah and the prophet Abinadi said that when Christ would "make his soul an offering for sin, he shall see his seed" (Isa. 53:10; compare Mosiah 15:10). Abinadi explains that "his seed" are the righteous, those who follow the prophets (see Mosiah 15:11). In the garden and on the cross, *Jesus saw each of us* and not only bore our sins, but also experienced our deepest feelings so that he would know how to comfort and strengthen us. . . .
>
> The Savior's atonement in the garden and on the cross is *intimate* as well as *infinite.* Infinite in that it spans the eternities. Intimate in that the Savior felt each person's pains, sufferings, and sicknesses. Consequently, he knows how to carry our sorrows and

relieve our burdens that we might be healed from within, made whole persons, and receive everlasting joy in his kingdom.[2]

"Years later, Elder Bateman taught:

> For many years I thought of the Savior's experience in the garden and on the cross as places where a large mass of sin was heaped upon Him. Through the words of Alma, Abinadi, Isaiah, and other prophets, however, my view has changed. Instead of an impersonal mass of sin, there was a long line of people, as Jesus felt "our infirmities" (Heb. 4:15), "[bore] our griefs, . . . carried our sorrows . . . [and] was bruised for our iniquities" (Isa. 53:4–5).
>
> The Atonement was an intimate, personal experience in which Jesus came to know how to help each of us.
>
> The Pearl of Great Price teaches that Moses was shown all the inhabitants of the earth, which were "numberless as the sand upon the sea shore" (Moses 1:28). If Moses beheld every soul, then it seems reasonable that the Creator of the universe has the power to become intimately acquainted with each of us. He learned about your weaknesses and mine. He experienced your pains and sufferings. He experienced mine. I testify that He knows us.[3]

"And for another witness, Elder John H. Groberg taught:

> I love the Savior. I feel that as he hung upon the cross and looked out over the dark scene, he saw more than mocking soldiers and cruel taunters. He saw more than crying women and fearful friends. He remembered and saw even more than women at wells or crowds on hills or throngs by seashores. He saw more, much more. He, who knows all and has all power, saw through the stream of time. His huge, magnanimous, loving soul encompassed all eternity and took in all people and all times and all sins and all forgiveness and all everything. *Yes, he saw down to you and to me* and provided us an all-encompassing opportunity to escape the terrible consequences of death and sin.[4]

"In the Book of Mormon, there is a phrase that always struck me," Bishop North said with a far-off look in his eyes. "As you know, after Jesus was crucified and resurrected, he visited a group of people in the Americas. As He came down in His glory, He invited the people to come and feel the wounds in His hands, feet, and side. The scriptures say that they came and touched Him 'one by one.' I've wondered how it was possible that it was one by one. I would imagine that in the crowd, one person would feel the wounds in His feet while another felt the wound in His side and yet another felt the wound in one of His hands. But instead, the scriptures say that it was one by one that they felt His wounds. I don't know if it is doctrine, Erica," Bishop North said, "but I've wondered if they experienced the Lord's wounds one by one because the converse was also true. I've wondered if Jesus suffered for each individual one by one and was wounded by each of us one by one.

"I do believe it was intimate," Bishop North went on. "In a terrifying way, I believe there was a name to each pain. And perhaps more than just a name in His mind, it was our image there. I believe that before His pure mind was all that we were, are, and ever would be. For how more intimately could anyone ever know another than when feeling every moment of suffering, sin, shame, pain, and sorrow in his or her life? At the time of the Atonement, no one could ever know another more deeply than Christ knew us there individually, exposed in our shame. And because the Lord's memory is perfect, He knows us better now than any other ever could or ever will."

"What else was in the cup?" Erica asked after some thought. "Besides sin?"

"We need to add pain to the cup," Bishop North replied. "The physical pains of every individual who has lived. But not just physical pains. Jesus suffered other types of pains, like we talked about before. As you know better than most, Erica, this life has pains that are more than just physical. There are also the pains of mistakes, regret, sadness, fear, loneliness, despair, rejection, and much more. We are talking about the pains of the emotionally and sexually abused, the lonely, and the suicidal. The cruel death of a loved one. All the sorrows and sufferings of this life, whether big or small, which are part of the very nature of this fallen world. Although this world is not hell in the scriptural sense, it sure can feel like it at times. To different degrees, each of us suffers a touch of hell in this life. And in the hours of Christ's sufferings, our agonies became His agony."

Erica didn't respond but stared at the red glow coming from one of the ovens' heating elements. She wondered if it were possible that Jesus suffered all that she had suffered. She thought of all the pain, the anger, and the times she had cried herself to sleep. "Why did Jesus have to suffer for more than just sin? Why suffer for other sorrows and inward pains?" Erica asked.

"So He could help carry our burdens and eventually heal us," the bishop responded. "Jesus not only restores us from sin, but He also heals us from the sins of others. Jesus wants to make you whole again, Erica. In Isaiah sixty-one, the scriptures talk about how He can give us 'beauty for ashes.' If we will come to Him, Jesus can take a destroyed life of ashes and restore it to a life that is whole and beautiful."

Erica's face looked grave as she sighed, thinking about all they had discussed. Then she thought about the night before. She thought about the things she had done with Steve. Her stomach churned in disgust over what she had allowed.

"I think I'm too far gone," Erica said as she set the measuring cup down and a tear ran down her cheek. "After the things I've done, I don't even think the Lord would want me. I've done things too awful to ever be forgiven."

"Do you know what dregs are?" Bishop North asked after some time in thought, picking up the cup Erica had set down.

"It's the grounds at the bottom of your coffee cup," Erica replied.

"Coffee, tea, hot chocolate, it doesn't matter," Bishop North said. "It's the thick stuff. The sediment that refuses to become part of the rest of the drink. It's the syrupy, turbid solution toward the bottom. In the scriptures it sometimes mentions the dregs of the bitter cup. If what Jesus suffered is symbolized by a bitter cup, then I've wondered what the dregs of that cup would be. I guess not all sin is created equally or is as repugnant as others. You said you thought that maybe you've gone too far," Bishop North said as he held up the large glass measuring cup. "That you're out of His reach. I guess that could be true if Jesus only partook of the top portion of the cup. I guess if Jesus only wanted to save those who would not sin *very bad* in the first place, He could have chosen to partake of the lighter things near the top, drinking only the top third of the cup. But instead, He drank to save us all. He suffered and drank the thick dregs at the bottom of the bitter cup. He finished the cup and left no sin or individual behind. He suffered all things so that He could save everyone. So no one could say, 'I'm out of His reach.' We can never go too far because there isn't any sin He did not willingly suffer for us."

"But how do you know He would even want me after the things I've done?" Erica asked in a cold, doubting voice.

"Remember, the Atonement was individual," Bishop North replied. "I suppose that as He was suffering for you or me, He could have stopped. He could have considered the cost too great for the person He was saving. But He didn't stop. Satan whispers lies into our ears. He wants us to think we've gone too far, that we are out of the Lord's reach or the Lord wouldn't want us, so why try anymore. But nothing could be further from the truth."

"How can you be so sure?" Erica asked.

"It's what the Lord does," Bishop North replied as he started to look in his scriptures. "All through scripture, the Lord has taken individuals who were lost and by His grace, changed them. For instance there was a man named Saul who was the foremost persecutor of the new Christian faith. He would throw members of the Church into prison and even have them put to death.[5] Imagine how the Savior would feel about people who have His humble followers put to death. But instead of letting the sword of justice fall on Saul, the Lord reached out and offered His grace. Later Saul began using the name Paul, and he wrote to his friend in 1 Timothy 1:15–16, explaining:

> Christ Jesus came into the world to save sinners; of whom I am chief. Howbeit for this cause I obtained mercy, that in me first Jesus Christ might shew forth all longsuffering, for a *pattern* to them which should hereafter believe on him to life everlasting.[6]

"In other words, the Lord reached out to Paul to give a teaching pattern for the rest of us. So we can say, 'If the Lord saved someone like that, then maybe He can save someone like me.' "

"It's hard to believe," Erica said. "I've given up on me, so why shouldn't He?"

The two of them sat there for a bit, and then Bishop North took off the watch on his wrist. "See this watch?" Bishop North held it up to her. "It's a pretty cheap watch. I think it cost me about fifteen dollars. If I broke the glass dial in front, how much do you think I would be willing to pay to fix it?"

"Not much," Erica replied. "It would probably cost you more

to fix it at a watch shop than you paid for it in the first place."

"I'm sure it would," Bishop North agreed. "But on the other hand, what if I had paid four hundred dollars for the watch? Do you think I would pay the thirty or forty dollars to have a four-hundred-dollar watch fixed?"

"I guess you probably would," Erica said.

"There's the principle," Bishop North said. "The more a person invests in something, the more they are willing to sacrifice to fix what's wrong. Because Jesus has put so much into us, He isn't going to waste all He has devoted to us when something goes wrong."

"But even if that were a four hundred dollar watch," Erica said, "if enough things started to go wrong with the watch, there would be a point that you would simply cut your losses. There would be a point that it wouldn't be worth it to fix. Maybe that's me. Maybe I have so many problems, I would just not be worth the trouble to Him."

"I guess all analogies break down at some point," Bishop North said. "We are much more personal to Him than watches. Also the difference is what Jesus has invested into you. It wasn't four hundred dollars; it was at an infinite cost that Jesus suffered and died for you. The Lord has put so much effort into us that He will not be willing to lose His investment when we start to make mistakes. Furthermore, Jesus did not just touch the agonies of our lives, He became engulfed in them—the agonies of souls and worlds without number. All these pains He suffered for us to demonstrate His love for us. Since it was an infinite amount He put into us, He will never give up on us. We may give up on ourselves, but He never will.

"He won't forget about us either," Bishop North went on. "I've seen you sometimes write things on your hands, Erica. Why do you do that?"

"They're reminders," Erica replied as she looked down on her palm and saw the remnants of black ink, left in the pores and lines of her hand. "Phone numbers and to-do lists."

"Why on your hands?" Bishop North asked.

"I guess I'll constantly see the messages there," Erica replied. "Why? Is it bad to write messages on yourself?"

"I'm not sure how to answer that," Bishop North said as he

opened his scriptures again. "But let me show you a scripture that might surprise you about why the Lord doesn't forget us. In Isaiah 49:15–16, it says:

> Can a woman forget her sucking child, that she should not have compassion on the son of her womb? yea, they may forget, yet will I not forget thee.

"And then the Lord says why He won't forget us:

> Behold, I have graven thee upon the palms of my hands; thy walls are continually before me.

"The Lord has also put reminders on His hands. Think of what the Lord is reminded of each time He looks down on His resurrected, glorified body. Not that the Lord needs reminders, but reminders is what He sees when He looks on the front and back of His hands. Reminders of His awful sufferings are continually before Him. He won't forget about you, Erica. And He won't give up on you. You cannot shock God by how badly you sin and fail in this life. When He came to you, to suffer for your sins, He knew what He was getting Himself into, and He loved you anyway. He knows exactly the shame of our sins and how badly we fail because He felt the exact shame we feel and chose to love us anyway. The Lord saw you there at your very worst and loved you so much He died so you can be healed and live."

Erica continued to look down at her own hands. She thought about the Lord's love and about Him looking out for her. "I want to live," Erica said in a broken voice. "I want to be a different, new person. I want to feel right."

"Then go to the Lord. Pray, ask for His mercy and a new life. He will be there for you, and He will show you the way."

NOTES

1. A few places where Jesus refers to His Atonement using the symbol of a cup are Matthew 26:39, 42; Mark 10:38; Mark 14:36; John 18:11; 3 Nephi 11:11; and D&C 19:18.
2. Elder Merrill J. Bateman's thoughts about the Atonement are found in his General Conference talk, "The Power to Heal from Within," *Ensign*, May 1995, 14 (emphasis added).

3. Merrill J. Bateman, "A Pattern for All," *Ensign*, Nov. 2005, 74.
4. Elder John H. Groberg's thoughts are found in "The Beauty and Importance of the Sacrament," *Ensign*, May 1989, 40 (emphasis added).
5. Some are surprised to find out that Paul was guilty of the great sin of murder. The references for this are Acts 7:57–60 and Acts 26:9–11.
6. Emphasis added.

chapter sixteen

ACTIONS' REACTIONS

Mitch couldn't sleep as long as usual on Saturday morning, so he went downstairs and poured himself his usual bowl of cereal and then wondered where Anna was.

"Morning," Anna said brightly as she came in the back door. Clearly she was out of breath, yet she had a smile of satisfaction on her face from the run she had just taken.

"Good morning," Mitch replied as he looked down in his bowl and sorted hardened marshmallows with his spoon. "Anna, what's going on?"

Anna stared at Mitch before answering. "I'm not sure what you mean."

"This just isn't you."

"I know," she said brightly as she got a bowl from the cupboard. "It's really not me. At least it's not the *me* I've been in a long time."

"Why are you doing this?" Mitch asked, contrasting her happiness with the negativity in his voice.

"I'm doing it because this is the person I've always wanted to be. That's what I love about it."

"What brought all this on?"

"You already know I've been talking with Bishop North," Anna said as she sat across from Mitch. "He's helped me see that the Lord has been very good to me. He said I need to show that same goodness to others in my life. That includes you, Mitch. I haven't always been the wife I planned on being for you."

"Then why the exercising and all the other things you're doing?" Mitch questioned.

"I didn't expect it," Anna said with some enthusiasm, "but since I started really trying to be gracious and good to others, it has had an overflowing effect in my life. It's made me want to show that same goodness to myself."

Mitch didn't respond but went back to spooning around his cereal.

"This change isn't easy, and I'm sure I'll often mess up," Anna said as she put her hand on Mitch's free hand. "But I feel like I'm being more of the person I've always wanted to be."

"I hope all this goes well for you," Mitch said awkwardly without looking up at Anna.

"For you too," Anna said as she squeezed Mitch's hand and then got up to leave Mitch in his thoughts.

"Mitch, it's a beautiful day out there," Anna declared from a back room. "Would you like to go for a walk with me? We can take Caitlin to the park."

"I think that could be good," he replied.

"I haven't been a very good person," Mitch said as he took in a large, trembling breath. There in the bishop's office, Mitch thought back on the last week. While Anna was happier than ever before, Mitch countered the balance by growing more miserable. Guilt and self-loathing had steadily been growing in his heart.

"Go on, Mitch," Bishop North said after waiting for almost a minute for Mitch to continue.

"About a year ago I started looking at things I shouldn't on the Internet," Mitch finally said. "It started out as looking at girls in bathing suits. At first I tried to justify it, thinking that it wasn't *that* bad. Most people wouldn't even really consider it pornography."

"It got worse, didn't it?" Bishop North wanted to stop Mitch and show him God's definition of pornography—anything that causes feelings of lust toward someone you aren't married to[1]—but he felt a prompting to refrain and allow Mitch to go on with his confession.

Mitch nodded his head as he looked up at the bishop for the first time and allowed the tears to break from his eyelids. "I'm an idiot, aren't I?"

Bishop North had never seen this side of Mitch before. But he had learned that being a bishop meant expecting the unexpected. "When is the last time you viewed any kind of pornography?" Bishop North asked, choosing to ignore Mitch's last question.

"I've been trying to stop," Mitch said. "More than ever, I don't want to be the person I've been."

"Mitch, how long has it been?"

"It's been four days," Mitch said. "I don't want to ever do that again."

"Is there more you need to confess?" Bishop North asked with a stern but hurt look on his face that he couldn't hide.

Mitch paused and then shook his head no.

"Mitch," Bishop North started, "in the short time I've been the bishop, I have noticed that a confession is a lot like opening an onion. You open it up, and you find there are layers. Sometimes once a person has made the huge leap of faith by coming willingly into the bishop's office, they make the mistake of only revealing the first couple of layers; partially confessing. You've done the hardest part—you're here, Mitch. If there is anything else, it will make repentance so much easier if you confess everything now."

Mitch said nothing. But where before Mitch avoided eye contact with the bishop, now he looked deeply into the bishop's eyes as if to read them. "Yeah, there is more. I have a lot of colleagues at work who are women. There is one that I've bantered back and forth with. A few months ago, it started to turn more toward flirting. I haven't actually done anything except . . ." Mitch paused again, thinking through what he might say. "Sometimes we've given each other hugs, an occasional touch on the hand, or a rub of the shoulders. I know it was progressing in a bad way. My thoughts haven't always been good either. That's pretty much the creep I've become."

"So then, what are you going to do, Mitch?" Bishop North asked. The question hung in the air as Mitch dropped his head back into his hands and rubbed his temples.

"I don't want to lose everything," Mitch responded as he looked in a far-off way out the window. "I don't want to lose

Anna. And we have barely been keeping our marriage together as it is. This information would be enough to end it. But something in the last few weeks has changed. I had forgotten how much I love her. When I was first getting to know her, something about her smile caught my heart. I remember thinking that if I could just always make her want to smile that smile, I would be the happiest man on earth. It had been a long time, and no thanks to me," Mitch added with a sigh, "but I've been seeing that smile more lately. Yet the happier she becomes and the nicer she becomes, the more I've been filled with guilt. I don't want to feel like this."

"How do you treat Anna?" Bishop North asked.

"I have often been pretty rough in the way I talk to her." Mitch said. "Whenever I've thought about it, I figured it was no big deal. But lately I've realized that I have been cruel to her. I think I've hurt her badly, at times, with the namecalling and the other things I've said over the years. I've also been really trying to speak differently to her lately."

"So what are you going to do, Mitch?" Bishop asked again.

"What do I need to do?"

"Are you willing to do anything I ask in order to save your marriage?" Bishop North asked.

"It's been awhile since I've looked at anything bad," Mitch defended. "I've been avoiding that woman at work. And like I said, I've been speaking differently to Anna."

"That's a good start, but what are you going to do to make sure you don't have those problems again?" Bishop North asked.

Then the two of them talked about the boundaries Mitch would need to set in order to avoid any degree or form of pornography. They also talked about the inappropriate relationship and more boundaries. Then they talked about the sacrament and the new heart Christ needed to make in Mitch.

"I'll do it, Bishop," Mitch said. "I'll do whatever it takes. I'll do anything to not lose Anna and my daughter. Like Anna, I want to be a better person. The person I always intended to be."

"Anna is the one you have hurt by your actions, Mitch," Bishop North said. "It's her you need to confess to."

"I'm pretty sure she has no idea about me looking at pornography," Mitch responded. "And I'm positive she doesn't know about the woman at work. Telling her would only hurt her more."

"The pornography and that relationship have already hurt her whether you realize it or not," Bishop North said. "There is no doubt that it has affected the way you have treated her. Mitch, you have already violated a great deal of the sacred trust between you two. She just doesn't know about it yet. In order to repent and really change, you need to tell her."

"I can't," Mitch said after a long silence, his chest starting to heave in and out. Mitch thought about the smile he committed himself to always help Anna have. He thought about the chaos and misery he had caused in their marriage. "I would rather do anything than hurt her like that."

"As hard as it is, I don't see any other way," Bishop North said.

"I'll change. More than ever, I'm committed to change everything. But I can't do that one thing. I would rather die than see the hurt it would cause her."

"I don't know of any other option," Bishop North said as he continued to feel the great weight of Mitch's sins. "Sin has its consequences. But those same consequences can help make sure that you never commit those sins again. If Anna and you are both willing, God can heal your marriage and make things right. But not without confession and true repentance. She has to know."

"Will you somehow tell her?" Mitch asked with a plea. "I know she would take it better from anyone but me. Would that satisfy what needs to be done?"

"I don't know," Bishop North said with feelings of frustration.

"Please!" Mitch begged. "I'll do everything and more. I'll treat her like a queen. I'll do anything, but just not that one thing."

"Hey," Anna said with a smile to her husband. "Thanks for fixing that chair."

"I guess I let that go long enough," Mitch replied.

"You've also been treating me differently. Thanks," Anna added, trying to act casual. But she knew that speaking with her husband like this was not the norm.

"Different in a good way?"

"Yeah," Anna said, mostly answering with her eyes and smile.

Anna leaned over and gave Mitch a kiss on the cheek and then went to sit at her computer.

"Dear Anna," she read as she started into her emails, seeing one from the bishop.

The other night, Mitch came in to talk to me. He asked that I tell you some things. Before telling you those things, I want to say that the grace and determination you have shown in loving Mitch has done so much. I can see that it is changing him. I have never known Mitch in the way that he and I spoke the other night. I hope you have also seen a change. Perhaps I've also been seeing more of the man you fell in love with.

As we talked, he spoke of his love for you and how he wanted to change. In part of that discussion he confessed to some serious sins. He understood that you needed to know this particular sin in order for the process of his repentance—and change—to really work and for it to last. He asked if I would tell you, and I reluctantly agreed.

In that interview he confessed to me that he had been viewing pornography on his laptop for over a year. He also said that he was determined to stop and he had not looked at any pornography for a few days prior to visiting me.

Anna read on about how the bishop felt he was going to change, but all she could feel was a sickness. She felt betrayed as she thought of him staring with lust at pictures of other women. She felt a vomiting anger rise up in her that made her feel nauseated as she read on. But then she felt another blow come:

Mitch also confessed that he had become flirtatious with a woman at work. He said that their relationship had gotten to the point of an occasional hug and shoulder rub but never more physical than that. I believe this is truly the case. Likewise, he has broken off all contact with this woman and expressed determination to—

Anna slowly stood and walked away, not caring to read the last paragraph of counsel from the bishop. Her mind was overflowing with thoughts and feelings of betrayal and hate. She thought of the other night when she and Mitch had been close together. Then she thought about how close he had been with this other woman. She coughed as bile came to her throat.

Mitch looked up from his book and saw Anna's eyes clenched in pain as she walked across the room toward the door.

"Anna," was all Mitch could say as the door slammed shut. He quickly got up and went to where his wife had been. There he saw Anna's computer with the bishop's email on the screen. Mitch crumbled to the floor. "Help us, Lord," he pled.

"I can't do this!" Anna said as she fell to her knees and continued her weeping. Through her tears and thoughts, she had driven to a nearby park where people rarely went. There, under a tree, she had fallen in her grief and despair.

"Why is this happening?" she continued as her fingers clenched down, digging into the dirt under the grass.

"Father," she prayed in a resentful tone. "I thought that grace would make things better. But it's all worse!" As Anna sat there in the grass, she envisioned image after image of Mitch flirting with some woman at work. She thought of the many times Mitch sat at his computer, probably looking at trashy women with lust in his heart. Anna thought of how he had treated her intimately and also how cruel his words had become. She threw a handful of sod. *What did I ever do to deserve to be treated like this?* Anna continued to think in her despair.

As the sun was setting and darkness was descending on the park, Anna took out the phone in her pocket.

"It's over, Bishop," Anna finally said. For a while, Anna could only hear her bishop sigh as he breathed out slowly.

"There's nothing worth saving," Anna continued rather than waiting for a response. "I want out."

"Anna," Bishop North said in a tender voice. "What if you could have your marriage like it once was?"

"It can *never* be like that again," Anna cried back. "There is no way it can now!"

"Doing the impossible is God's specialty," Bishop North reminded.

"But what you are asking me to do is unrealistic," Anna

replied. "It's not practical! I can't do it."

"I really believe that Mitch is committed to trying to make things work, Anna. Look how he has been the last few days," Bishop North offered.

"That's because he's the one who screwed up!" Anna said, louder than she intended to speak at the park. "Maybe he confessed this just to extinguish any happiness I was beginning to feel in my life."

"Anna, I know if you will try, the Lord will heal your relationship," Bishop North said in a much calmer voice. "Maybe even better than you could imagine."

"Why are you doing this to me?" Anna sobbed quietly into the phone.

"The Lord loves you, Anna. He just wants you to have a happy, good life. Keep showing Mitch that grace that God has shown to you. Do good to, and pray for, those who hurt you."

Anna pondered how she was supposed to act. She thought of how she was supposed to show love to Mitch. "I just can't do what you are asking," Anna said after some time.

"I'm not the one asking you to do anything, Anna," Bishop North responded. "It's what the Lord is asking of you."

"Then what the Lord is asking is beyond me. I just don't have it in me. I don't have that much grace in me. I'm going to go to my sister's house," Anna said in conclusion.

"Let me just ask one last thing of you, Anna. There is an aspect of grace you haven't heard yet. There's something we haven't talked about that you need to hear. Please come to my office tomorrow night. There is a way and there is still hope."

NOTE

1. God's definition of pornography, or perversion of what we look at, is in Doctrine and Covenants 42:22–23, "Thou shalt love thy wife with all thy heart, and shalt cleave unto her and none else. And he that looketh upon a woman to lust after her shall deny the faith, and shall not have the Spirit; and if he repents not he shall be cast out."

chapter seventeen

LIGHT AND DARKNESS

As Bishop North opened the door to his bakery in the early morning hours, he saw a note from Erica that had been slid under the door.

Bishop North,

Right now my palms are sweaty, my heart is racing, and I want to scream and die at the same time. I can't deal with this. The only reason I can even write to you right now is because, as you know from seeing my notebooks, writing is about the only way I know how to deal with things.

After talking with you the other day, I went home and my old boyfriend that I used to be with was still there. In fact, I had done some bad things with him only the night before we talked last. But after we talked, I was feeling different. I told him to leave. After he left I started to look over the last ten years of my life. There has hardly been a sin I haven't committed in that time. Maybe it's no surprise to you, but I've practically done them all. But as I looked over my life, I saw nothing of worth in any of those things. I saw that there were moments of pleasure, but no matter what it was, it soon got old and I found my heart and soul more empty and cold from every experience.

Then I thought over the time I've known you and how you have always had purpose and determination. You have always had a secret satisfaction and joy in life that has impressed me. It's part of the reason I have stayed working for you over these years. You seem to have a purpose and something worthwhile in your life.

Then I remembered that when we talked last, you said the Lord could heal me and give me a new life; you said the Lord would show me mercy, and He would become part of my life.

I kneeled down and prayed. I asked for forgiveness and asked the Lord to make me into a new person. I committed my life to doing what He wants me to do. Slowly I felt my empty soul begin to fill with light. Nothing in this world could feel as good as I was feeling then. It was as if heaven and God's presence had come into me. Tears of joy and peace flowed down. I was filled with light and an excitement that I was going to try to live my life the way God wanted me to.

But as it always is with me, the good feelings couldn't last. It's as if it wasn't meant to be. The next morning I still felt good. Then I saw the mail my roommate left from the day before. There was a letter from my mom. Inside was a document from the state explaining that Dean, the man who had hurt me, was going to be released from prison early for "good behavior" and that he was planning to relocate in this area. I can't deal with that, Bishop! I cannot begin to explain the feelings I have been having since then. It has brought up everything from the past. I've been tied up in fear and anger.

For years I've been tormented with the memories of what he did. At any given moment, I would imagine myself doing something to hurt or even kill him. I've imagined myself stabbing him in his sleep. It's been years since it happened. Yet I speculate that if I could have told someone earlier or if I had fought him, it would have been different. I want to leave it alone and forget what he did to me, but it's like he's still hurting me. I had some relief once he was sentenced to prison, but it seems like I've been the one who has been tortured in a different type of prison.

It has only been in the last couple of years that I have been able to move on a bit, but with that letter I got, all the agony is back!

I want to live a new life, but maybe this misery is my fate. Maybe it's just what's meant to be.

Sorry to drop all this on you. But I also wanted you to

know that I won't be here for my shift this afternoon. Sorry to bring you into any of this. Maybe the only solution is for me to go away entirely.

Erica

chapter eighteen

CONTEMPLATIONS

"Deborah!" Ken gasped in horror as he came into the closet of their master bedroom. There Deborah sat on the chair with a look of quiet contemplation on her face. But in her hand she held Ken's large handgun.

"What are you doing?" Ken asked in unbelief.

"Where's the key to the gun's safety?" She asked in a stoic voice, without looking up. "You used to keep it on that top shelf, but it's not there now."

"Deborah, stop this."

"I'm trying to," Deborah replied quietly. "Just tell me where you keep the key now and walk away. Tell me, and you will never have to worry about me again. All I ask is that you don't let the kids know how it happened, just—"

"Deborah!" Ken said, raising his voice. "I can't let—"

"Yes, you can," Deborah interrupted, still focusing on the gun. "The girls are young, and I know you've always been able to get them to believe whatever you want. You're a smart man."

"No," Ken replied softly, but even as the words left his mouth he considered the possibility of what she was requesting. Thoughts raced before his mind. The months of coldness between them. Misery. Resentment. Happy years, and Deborah's warm touch. Jimmy's body floating in the water. His secretary's touch. Nights hearing his wife's sobs of pain.

"You can't do this. I won't let you," Ken said as he stepped forward, pulled the gun from her hands, and then started out of the large closet.

"Ken," Deborah said, stopping him in the doorway. "Did you do that because you love me or out of some duty?"

Ken stood there but refused to look back. "Don't worry, I know the answer," she said.

"I don't want it to be like this," Ken said after a long silence. "We had a good life before, didn't we?"

"It doesn't matter," she replied. "It's gone."

"The kids need you," Ken tried.

"They really don't," she declared. "And neither do you."

chapter nineteen

EMPTY

There was a quiet, solemn feeling in the room as Erica, Anna, and Ken came into Bishop North's office again. As he thanked each for coming, Bishop North looked around to see each person's expression that reflected the deep pain and sorrow they carried. "As a bishop, I know a good deal about what each of you are going through, while others here may not know of each other's pains at all. But I just thought that—"

"I'll start," Ken interrupted.

"Hold on," Bishop North said, stopping Ken from saying more. "Before you say anything, I didn't mean for anyone to feel like they need to share. I don't know if it would be wise for all of us to confess every detail of what we're going through to each other."

"Each of you can do what you like," Ken said to the other two. "But I would rather you know about the issues in my life. A lot of you probably already know."

"Go ahead then, Ken," Bishop North said reluctantly. "But be careful."

"As most of you know, just over a year ago, our son Jimmy almost drowned in our backyard swimming pool. Jimmy suffered a great deal of brain damage and will be in a wheelchair, mentally impaired, for the rest of his life. Deborah and I had a good life and relationship before the accident. But since then. . ." Ken paused, searching for the words. "She has changed, and so have I. The truth is that I haven't been able to forgive her in my heart. I can't seem to help but blame her for what happened. I'm sure it was an accident, and she just forgot about looking after Jimmy, but that mistake has shattered everything in my life."

"Then a couple of days ago, I came into our walk-in closet and found my wife with my handgun, trying to take her life," Ken said as he brought his hands up and covered his clenched expression. "As I've told the bishop, I don't know what to do, but things can't remain the way they are. I have to . . . I want to forgive her. But I just don't know how. I'm empty inside. I just don't have anything left in me."

No one said anything for a minute until Anna spoke up. "I guess my situation has some similarities but is also different. Our marriage has been struggling. I'm not sure if Mitch and I ever really had many good times like you mentioned," Anna said while looking over at Ken. "But I've realized that it hasn't all been his fault. Like Bishop North encouraged us, in the last couple of weeks, I've tried to show grace and goodness to my husband, Mitch. In that time I started to see a change for good in our relationship. I felt hope for us for the first time in years. But now everything has been torn apart. Without going into all the details, I've just learned that Mitch has been unfaithful to me, and he wants my forgiveness. I want a good marriage, but I'm so angry with him. I don't see how I could ever love him again or forgive him." Though she tried to hide it when the group's eyes were on her, Anna's expression showed the anger and resentment she felt.

"Here's my story," Erica started. The rest of the group was somewhat surprised. Until now Erica had said very little when they had met.

"You don't have to," Bishop North interjected kindly.

"I know," Erica said. "But I feel like I really want to."

"Everything's private here," Anna said as she laid a comforting hand on Erica's back. It actually felt good to Erica, helping her realize that she wasn't the only one struggling.

"I was in the sixth grade when my mom remarried. Like any kid, I dreamed of a normal family like other kids had. Then my stepdad started to do things to me," Erica said and then paused. "For over a year, he repeatedly molested me and raped me. My life has been pretty messed up. After that I gave up on God. I've worked for Bishop North for a couple of years now, and he has been good to me. He's even helped me see that God still loves me. Recently, life has felt as if it was getting better, and I was moving on with life. Then almost on cue, I got a letter from the state saying how the man who raped me will be released from prison and will be relocating here in the city. All the anger and issues that I've bottled up and pushed deep down have come back to the top with a vengeance. I feel like I can't live like this," Erica said with finality. "I can't live with him out there. I could barely keep things together when he was in prison."

Bishop North looked over the three of them and wondered if they were ready for what he was about to say. He wondered if they were ready to learn some very difficult ideas. But as he looked, he saw three individuals, not just at the breaking point, but who had been broken in their hearts.

"You three have expressed awful challenges," Bishop North started. "You've mentioned feeling empty and that you can't live your lives the way they are anymore. In some ways, maybe those are good things. Often God can renovate a person's life better when they are at this point than at any other time."

"What do you mean?" Anna asked with some disdain. "God wants us like this?"

"Sometimes, in order for God to heal us," Bishop North replied. "He has to break us first. In order for God to fill us, He first has to empty us."

"I really have no idea what you are talking about," Anna said in a quiet and serious tone.

"I know each of you are going through very difficult things right now, and I want you to know that there is hope for better things," Bishop North said, continuing on. "But before we dive into everything, there is a principle that we need to learn before all others. It's a gatekeeper principle—a key principle that when understood, opens our understanding to many other critical things. This principle lays the foundation and makes real forgiveness and humility possible."

"Okay, Bishop," Ken said for the group but with no energy in his voice. "I think we're all ready then."

"I've prepared quite a few things, but the first is a quote that struck me the first time I heard it and clarified a few things for me," Bishop North said. "The first time Elder Neil L. Andersen spoke as a new apostle in conference, he said:

> Just after my call as a General Authority 16 years ago, in a stake conference where I accompanied President Boyd K. Packer, he said something I have not forgotten. As he addressed the congregation, he said, "I know who I am." Then after a pause, he added, "I am a nobody." He then turned to me, sitting on the stand behind him, and said, "And, Brother Andersen, you are a nobody too." Then he added these words: "If you ever forget it, the Lord will remind you of it instantly, and it won't be pleasant."[1]

"What is this then?" Bishop North questioned the group. "Is this a new gospel principle? That we are to think of ourselves as being nobodies?"

"I've always been taught that I was of 'infinite worth,' " Anna responded to the seemingly rhetorical question. "I remember that from Young Women."

"So which is it then? Are we of infinite worth or are we nothing?" Bishop North asked, building on her response. "How could both be true?"

"It doesn't seem possible to be of infinite worth and worthless at the same time," Ken said to the group.

"But I want to show you that both are very true," Bishop North replied with a smile. "We are of infinite worth, yet nobodies at the same time. We will dig into both of these ideas," Bishop North said. "We'll look together at our nothingness and then our great worth.

"First, let's look at our ultimate example," Bishop North said, "our Lord Jesus Christ. In the New Testament, there is a story of a rich young ruler who came to Jesus." Bishop North turned pages in his scriptures. "In Mark 10, verses 17 and 18, it says:

> And when he was gone forth into the way, there came one running, and kneeled to him, and asked him, Good Master, what shall I do that I may inherit eternal life?
>
> And Jesus said unto him, Why callest thou me good? there is none good but one, that is, God.

"Then Jesus went on and helped the young man see what he needed to do to have eternal life. But let's focus on his initial response. That story is told three times in the scriptures, and each time the Lord's response is the same, saying that there is none good but God. Is Jesus not good? There is no Joseph Smith Translation or some other clarification. But is Jesus just giving us 'false modesty' here? Like when a lovely teenage girl says she's not pretty?"

"That can't be," Ken scowled. "I don't think Jesus would ever say something not true, especially just to appear humble."

"Then what is humility?" Bishop North asked.

"It's the opposite of pride," Anna responded.

"Then what's pride?" Bishop North dug further.

"Pride is to think you're better than others," Anna said.

"Then if humility is the opposite of pride," Bishop North said, "What does that make humility?"

"To think you're worse than others?" Ken responded in a questioning tone. "I don't know about that. Surely Jesus is honestly better than us all."

"That's very true," Bishop North confirmed. "Jesus is better than any of us. But that is not the relationship that the Savior chose to focus on during His mortal life. Rather than constantly comparing Himself to other people, Jesus's focus was always on the Father. Likewise Jesus challenged all to 'learn of me; for I am meek and lowly in heart.'[2] Jesus could say this because Jesus rightly saw the Father as the source of all goodness that He had obtained. Jesus worshiped the Father and took upon Himself the status of a servant to His Father.[3] He was constantly attributing every righteous word and act to His Father,[4] always directing the praise to God. In all honesty, Jesus truly saw that there was only one that was good, and that was God.

"This is also how the prophets and all of God's people have eventually thought of themselves," Bishop North continued. "King Benjamin told his people that he was no better than they were. The same Ammon that cut off the arms of the attacking Lamanites and converted thousands said, "Yea, I know that I am nothing; as to my strength I am weak; therefore I will not boast of myself, but I will boast of my God, for in his strength I can do all things."[5]

"What's the value in this?" Ken questioned Bishop North in a frustrated tone of voice. "Even if it is true that we are nothing, I can't see why God would remind us of our nothingness. Why would the Lord want us to always remember that we are nothing? Why would He want us to be self deprecating?"

"I've thought quite a bit about that very question," Bishop North said in a serious voice. "I've thought of four valuable reasons why the Lord would want us to always realize our nothingness. The first reason is that realizing our fallen state is essential to true conversion to God." Bishop North leaned over and grabbed a paper with a quote on it from his desk. "President Ezra Taft Benson stated that:

> Just as a man does not really desire food until he is hungry, so he does not desire the salvation of Christ until he knows why he needs Christ.
>
> No one adequately and properly knows why he needs Christ until he understands and accepts the doctrine of the Fall and its effect upon all mankind.[6]

"Likewise, King Benjamin's people were not wicked by most standards, but it was not until after King Benjamin helped them realize their 'nothingness' and see their 'worthless and fallen state' that they had 'no more disposition to do evil, but to do good continually.' It wasn't until after they saw themselves as 'beggars,' 'dust,' 'indebted,' and 'unprofitable servants' that they cried out to God and had their mighty conversion. So the first reason to remember our nothingness is that it leads to true conversion. Like we said before, we need to be broken and emptied before we can have the Lord heal and fill us. Realizing our nothingness will cause us to look up to God, for there is none other to look to. Since He is the only one that is good, He becomes our full view.

"A second reason it is important to recognize our nothingness," Bishop North went on, "is it makes us into more powerful disciples. There is power in honestly seeing ourselves as weak."

"What do you mean?" Ken interjected. "How can being weak be a good thing?"

"Great question," Bishop North responded. "Realizing our weakness drives us to seek the real source of all power." Bishop North picked up his scriptures again and went to some bookmarks he had inserted. "The Apostle Paul, after talking about a great affliction he carried in life, said in 2 Corinthians 12:8–10:

> For this thing I besought the Lord thrice, that it might depart from me.

> And he said unto me, My grace is sufficient for thee: for my strength is made perfect in weakness. Most gladly therefore will I rather glory in my infirmities, that the power of Christ may rest upon me.
>
> Therefore I take pleasure in infirmities, in reproaches, in necessities, in persecutions, in distresses for Christ's sake: for when I am weak, then am I strong.

"Isn't it remarkable that Paul was actually rejoicing that the Lord had given him obvious weaknesses? Likewise, after Moroni was considering his weaknesses, the Lord said in Ether 12:27:

> And if men come unto me I will show unto them their weakness. I give unto men weakness that they may be humble; and my grace is sufficient for all men that humble themselves before me; for if they humble themselves before me, and have faith in me, then will I make weak things become strong unto them.

"Before miraculous experiences, there is a common pattern in scriptures of first recognizing one's own nothingness and weaknesses. Before Jacob, in Genesis 32, had his grand vision and was blessed by God, he prayed unto the Lord, 'I am not worthy of the least of all the mercies, and of all the truth, which thou hast shewed unto thy servant.' Before the Lord touched the clear stones of the Brother of Jared and appeared in glory, the Brother of Jared had first prayed a prayer of abject humility, expressing his iniquity, unworthiness, weakness, and fallen nature. Then he pled for the Lord's pity and mercy. It was the Brother of Jared's great humility that gave him the faith to behold the Lord. If when we see we are weak, we will become strong, then what does that say about when we see ourselves as strong?"

"We'll become weak?" Anna asked.

"Yes," Bishop North said. "Confidence in our own abilities and strengths will eventually make us weak. As a bishop, when I've counseled people who have fallen into sin, I've seen that there is often a pattern of overconfidence. They felt that because they were spiritually mature, or because they were a returned missionary, they were strong enough not to fall into certain sins. They thought, 'I can handle it.' But the moment they felt they were strong enough, sin started to creep into their lives. Someone scared of sin is much less likely to fall than someone who is fearless. Same with a new driver. As soon as they become confident in their driving abilities, they are poised for an accident.

"There was a young lady I knew, and whenever she went out on a date or out with friends, instead of her parents saying, 'Return with honor' or 'Remember who you are,' they would say, 'Remember, Kelly, you're not special.' You would think that this would make her feel bad about herself, but instead, you could hardly find a happier person. What they meant by the saying was, 'Remember, Kelly, *when it comes to sin*, you're not special.' They wanted her to know that she could slip up as easily as anyone else, so she needed to beware."

"Now this third reason might be hard to believe," Bishop North said, "but the next reason it is important to recognize our nothingness is it helps us to be happier people."

"That would be the last thing I would think of," Anna said with a laugh. "From what you're saying, it seems as if the Lord wants us to see our nothingness and then He would want to see us moaning and lamenting our pathetic selves."

"But strangely," Bishop North said with a smile, "just the opposite is true. In King Benjamin's address, he gave a formula for how to 'always rejoice' and 'be filled with the love of God.' Look for the surprising things he says we need to do to find this joy in life in Mosiah 4:11–12:

> And again I say unto you as I have said before, that as ye have come to the knowledge of the glory of God, or if ye have known of his goodness and have tasted of his love, and have received a remission of your sins, which causeth such exceedingly great joy in your souls, even so I would that ye should remember, and always retain in remembrance, the greatness of God, and your own nothingness, and his goodness and long-suffering toward you, unworthy creatures, and humble yourselves even in the depths of humility, calling on the name of the Lord daily, and standing steadfastly in the faith of that which is to come, which was spoken by the mouth of the angel.
>
> And behold, I say unto you that if ye do this ye shall always rejoice, and be filled with the love of God, and always retain a remission of your sins; and ye shall grow in the knowledge of the glory of him that created you, or in the knowledge of that which is just and true.

"Isn't that strange that by always remembering God's greatness and our nothingness, that by seeing ourselves as unworthy creatures compared to His goodness, it will help us to 'always rejoice'?"

"That goes against everything I've ever believed about happiness," Anna said.

"Well, what does the world teach is the way to be happy?" Bishop North questioned.

"You need to think highly of yourself," Anna replied. "You need to have high self-esteem."

"What do you do to think highly of yourself?" Bishop North questioned further.

"I don't know," Anna started. "Maybe by being really good at something, positive self-talk, or having success or achievements."

"Does it work?" Bishop North asked.

"It does feel good to accomplish goals or to be successful." Anna assured him.

"How long does that happiness last?"

"About as long as it takes to compare yourself to someone better," Ken stepped in. "Over my life, I've found it doesn't last terribly long. Success is insatiable. You always want more."

"Isn't it strange," Bishop North said, "to the world, the secret to happiness is to esteem yourself highly. While King Benjamin said the key to happiness is to esteem *God* highly. Maybe it is like that scripture in Matthew 16, 'For whosoever will save his life shall lose it: and whosoever will lose his life for my sake shall find it.' The person trying to find himself—and live for himself—never finds the peace and fulfillment he desires. But the person who loses himself and instead lives for the Lord, he finds joy and satisfaction from life."

Bishop North grabbed another paper from the same stack on his desk. "Speaking about the joy of having this humility with God, C. S. Lewis wrote:

> He and you are two things of such a kind that if you really get into any kind of touch with Him you will, in fact, be humble—delightedly humble, feeling the infinite relief of having for once got rid of all the silly nonsense about your own dignity which has made you restless and unhappy all your life. He is trying to make you humble in order to make this moment possible: trying

> to take off a lot of silly, ugly, fancy-dress in which we have all got ourselves up and are strutting about like the little idiots we are. I wish I had got a bit further with humility myself: if I had, I could probably tell you more about the relief, the comfort, of taking the fancy-dress off—getting rid of the false self, with all its "Look at me" and "Aren't I a good boy?" and all its posing and posturing. To get even near it, even for a moment, is like a drink of cold water to a man in a desert.[7]

"I want you to know that God desires our happiness. Although it may not make sense to the world, I can speak from personal experience that King Benjamin is right: realizing our nothingness and focusing on God's great goodness brings lasting joy in life.

"A fourth reason it is crucial to recognize our nothingness is that it is the only way to destroy the great sin of pride," Bishop North said. "Pride and humility are on opposite sides of the spectrum. *Acting* humble isn't a solution to pride. We actually have to *be* humble. The scriptures say that 'he that exalteth himself shall be abased, and he that abaseth himself shall be exalted.'[8] Pride is trying to exalt ourselves above others while abasing is the lowering of ourselves."

"I'm not sure of that connection," Ken said. "Why would thinking less of myself affect how I think of others?"

"The answer is in the Book of James," Bishop North said, turning in his scriptures. "In the beginning of chapter 2, James is teaching that we shouldn't treat some people better than others. Then in verse 10, he gives the most powerful reason why:

> For whosoever shall keep the whole law, and yet offend in one point, he is guilty of all.

"In other words, let's say that you were able to keep all of the laws of God perfectly all of the time except you made a mistake in just one point of the law. Then that makes you guilty of breaking the laws of God as a whole."

"Wait," Ken objected. "Breaking one commandment doesn't make me guilty of breaking all of them."

"Right," Bishop North agreed. "But in God's eyes it really boils down to two types of people. Those who have broken God's laws, and those who have not sinned. Like it says in Romans 3:23, 'all have sinned, and come short of the glory of God.' So on the one side is Jesus, who lived perfectly. And all of the rest of the human family falls on the other side. So do you see why James is saying we shouldn't treat some better than others?"

"Because we are all in the same boat," Anna answered. "He's saying we all need God's goodness and mercy."

"That's right," Bishop North said in a subdued voice. "We all desperately need His grace to be saved, so who are we to ever think we are better than other people who need God's grace. Like King Benjamin said, we are all beggars before God. So wouldn't it be silly for one beggar to say to another, 'Hey, the cardboard box I sleep in is much better than your box,' when in reality, they are both beggars needing help? Essentially, we are no better than anyone else. The only one who is truly good is God."

"So by truly realizing I'm a beggar before God, like everyone else," Ken said, "that will end my pride?"

"Yeah," Bishop North said with a half smile. "Like Anna said, we are all in the same boat. And it is such a relief to be able to finally let go of our pride. Have you ever wondered why people often like to hold others' mistakes over their heads? It's pride. When people see they can't become better than another person in one area, they try to tear that person down in another area to compensate. They want to create some area that they are better than the other person so they refuse to forgive. They try to bring themselves up by cutting others down. And thus, in our pride, as we try to control and hold people accountable to us, we become bitter, sad, angry people. In an argument, which bothers you more?" Bishop North asked. "Someone else being right and you wrong, or them *thinking* they are right and you are wrong?

"So how can we overcome such chaos?" Bishop North asked rhetorically. "Surrender. Give up the competition. We have to realize that despite what many think, we are all on the same playing field. We are all beggars. Again, Jesus expressed this thought best when He said, 'There is only one that is good, that is God.' Once we see ourselves as nothing and God as everything, we can finally start to treat others in the way God would have us treat them. Finally, it enables us to stop fostering our pride and to show true kindness. We can finally start to love others. By realizing our own nothingness, we finally surrender the unyielding battle of always trying to be better than others. Our joy isn't based on being better than others. Instead our joy is based on Christ. Considering ourselves to be beggars before God makes it possible for us to do great kindnesses to others. For Jesus it was the same way. His true humility is what made it possible for Him to take on the role of a lowly servant and wash the Apostles' feet. Jesus was not in the competition we humans often try to run with each other. He only focused on His Father's goodness and tried to please Him. He only cared what His Father thought of Him."

"Okay, we are nothing," Anna stated. "But if I'm just nothing, I don't see how very much happiness in life is possible. You also said we were of infinite worth. How can that be?"

NOTES

1. Neil L. Andersen, "Come unto Him," *Ensign*, May 2009, 78–80.
2. Matthew 11:29
3. Philippians 2:6–7
4. John 5:19 and John 8:28–29
5. Alma 26:12
6. Ezra Taft Benson, "The Book of Mormon and the Doctrine and Covenants," *Ensign*, May 1987, 83.
7. C. S. Lewis, *Mere Christianity* (New York: Macmillan, 1952), 114.
8. Doctrine and Covenants 101:42

chapter twenty

INFINITE WORTH

"It's a good question," Ken added. "Are we of infinite worth or worthless? I don't think we can be both."

"Worth," Bishop North said. "It's a curious concept. Do you know how worth is determined?"

The group answered by their silence.

"Sometimes we think that worth is determined by some inherent value found in an object. But the truth is, worth changes constantly in this world. For instance, gold is often thought of as a stable commodity, but its dollar value changes daily on the world's markets. In fact, under the right circumstances, a cup of water could become far more valuable than gold."

"Then how is worth of anything ever determined?" Anna questioned.

"One factor, and one factor only, determines the worth of anything," Bishop North replied. "Worth is determined by how much someone is willing to pay for that object. For instance, a gas generator that someone bought for a few hundred dollars could become worth a few thousand dollars in an ice storm.

"That brings up another interesting point about worth," Bishop North continued. "Worth is always determined by the highest bidder. Art is an example of this idea. Someone might be willing to pay thousands of dollars for a piece of art that someone else might consider trash. Yet the worth of the item has then been set by that highest bidder. Consider how a baseball can also be an example of this principle. At the store, you can buy a good baseball for a few dollars, but the worth of the ball can change dramatically by what happens to it. A few years ago, Mark McGwire hit his seventieth home run in a single season, breaking a tremendous record. The fan that caught the home run ball turned around and auctioned the ball for two million dollars. What then is the worth of the ball? Regardless of how much *we* might be willing to pay for the ball, the worth is two million dollars because that is what someone willingly paid."

"But a person's worth isn't determined like that," Anna objected.

"Isn't it?" Ken said. "If a person is talented or beautiful, don't we as a society decide they are of great worth? If a person invents something special or can shoot three-pointers all day long with a basketball, don't we pay them gobs of money for their skills?"

"Sadly he's right," Bishop North said. "And on the other hand, how does the world's system of assigning worth deal with those who are poor, disabled, unskilled, mentally handicapped, or less than beautiful? They become the leftover baggage of the world. With the world's way of seeing worth, societies can become awful places. People start thinking with a Darwinian philosophy of 'survival of the fittest.' In Nazi Germany, as Hitler came into power, the first individuals he started to do away with were not the Jews or Gypsies. The first ones he went after were the institutionalized: all those in state facilities for the disabled and mentally ill. He saw these needy people as leeches on society, sapping its strength. So they were disposed of."

"But our society isn't like that," Anna objected again. "We take care of the poor and create special programs to accommodate those with handicaps or disabilities."

"And why are we like that?" Bishop North questioned. "It's because God has declared each individual of infinite worth, and so many in our society see things the same way."

"So everyone is of worth just because God said we were?" Erica questioned.

"Not quite," Bishop North replied. "Remember that what determines the worth of anything is what someone pays for that thing. So then, how much did the Lord pay for us? In Gethsemane and on the cross, the Lord suffered for each individual, the millionaire down to the bum on the street, begging for money. The Lord's sufferings, His pain, His trembling body, the blood He bled, were given in an infinite amount for each individual. The Book of Mormon describes Christ's payment for sin as an 'infinite atonement.'[1] Therefore, as

Christ paid an infinite price for you, that became your worth."

"But what if the world says a person has no worth, but God says they are of infinite worth?" Erica asked. "Who's right? Is it just a matter of opinion?"

"There we go back to that other fixed principle," Bishop North said. "Worth is always determined by the *highest* amount paid. In other words, the highest bidder always determines worth. So if the Lord says that we are of infinite worth, and by His own blood paid that price, but others say we are not worth much, the true worth goes to that highest bid. The Lord's determination of worth isn't right just because He is God but because that was the highest price paid.

"Still, as mortals, there are two ways of determining worth. We can choose to calculate others' worth correctly, based on how Christ has determined their worth, or we can assign worth as the world does. If we pick God's way of thinking of worth, then we can understand that the poor and those in need are of worth, not because they have contributed so much, in a cold, literal sense, but based on the sacrifice of Jesus Christ.

"On the other hand, if we take God out of our perspective, then didn't Hitler have the right idea? He saw the destitute as people who were contributing nothing to the society while draining the resources of the community.

"If we see worth God's way, then the world is a beautiful place of kindness, concern, and love. If we see worth without God's perspective, the world is a sad, cold, and dark place. In the world's eyes, it seems impractical to love others and value them this way. The showing of this grace to the needy makes little sense to the world. But to God's people, it's fundamental.

"This is also why almost all of the charitable organizations in the world are run and funded by God-fearing people. Because of the love that God showed through His Son and the love that is still in the world, people do find others to be of worth, regardless of ability, appearance, power, or money. There are still those who strive to help the destitute, the lonely, the hurt, and the disabled. There are those in the world who try to love each individual as Christ would, not because the world finds them of worth, but because Christ has given the final verdict: each person is of infinite worth. The worth of souls is truly great in the sight of God, and we do not see people correctly until we see them as being of infinite worth as the Lord does."

"Okay, maybe I'm just slow," Anna said with a hint of frustration. "But which is it? Are we 'less than the dust of the earth' like King Benjamin said, or are we of 'infinite worth' like you are now saying?"

"Yes," Bishop North said, smiling, "to both ends of your question. We are of infinite worth, Anna, but lest our heads grow too big, we should be sure to understand we are of worth not because of *our* goodness but because of *His* ultimate goodness and sacrifice. Without question, we are of infinite worth, and yet of ourselves, we have nothing to boast about. Without Christ we are nothing and are less than the dust of the earth. Our value is not based on how good-looking we are, how talented we are, or even how good we are at doing what is right. Christ, and all that He suffered and paid for us, determines our value. If we are left to ourselves, we can only conclude that we are nothing. Even all the good we may accomplish is due to the Lord's great work in our lives, for which He deserves the ultimate credit.

"For instance, after Ammon and his brothers had performed the great miracles of converting the Lamanites to the gospel, Ammon's brother thought he was boasting," Bishop North said as he turned in his Book of Mormon. "To this Ammon said:

> Yea, I know that I am nothing; as to my strength I am weak; therefore I will not boast of myself, but I will boast of my God, for in his strength I can do all things; yea, behold, many mighty miracles we have wrought in this land, for which we will praise his name forever.

"Notice how Ammon said he was 'nothing' and 'weak.' Ammon's joy was in the great work God did and that he was able to participate in that.

"It's kind of like the newborn son of a king," Bishop North said. "Is that prince of great worth because of what he accomplished?"

"No," Ken replied. "It's who his father is that makes him great."

"So it is with us," Bishop North added. "It's who our Father in Heaven is that makes us great and of infinite worth."

NOTE

1. See 2 Nephi 9:7 and Alma 34:12

chapter twenty-one

FORGIVENESS

"FORGIVENESS IS SURRENDERING MY RIGHT TO HURT YOU FOR HURTING ME."

—Archibald Hart

"I mentioned before that understanding humility and the fact that we are all in need of grace are gatekeeper principles," Bishop North said. "We need to understand our nothingness before we get to the heart of the matter: forgiveness."

Anna, Erica, and Ken each thought about their own struggles to forgive. Anna thought of her great collapse in trusting Mitch after learning of his flirtatious relationship with a woman at work and also his problem with pornography. Anna's stomach tightened. Then she thought about how she had also made mistakes. She thought about how in God's eyes, she too was in need of His grace.

Erica thought of her former stepfather who had hurt her. She thought of her supposed nothingness that Bishop North had taught and then Dean's nothingness. It seemed so different.

Ken thought of the anger he had fostered for all these months against Deborah. *Am I also just as guilty in God's eyes?* he thought to himself. He thought back on that fateful evening when he had come home late and found his drowning son. *"What if I hadn't come home late? What if I went and found my kids right away? Is this just as much my fault?* Ken thought of his wife sitting there with his gun. He thought of Jimmy in his wheelchair. Guilt gripped his heart. *What have I done? Help me, Lord.*

"Someday when we stand before God, do we want justice or mercy from God?" Bishop North asked.

"I think I want mercy," Ken said softly.

"Justice too," Anna said, looking over at Ken with surprise. "We want justice *and* mercy, don't we?"

"The role of justice can be surprising when we look at it scripturally," Bishop North said as he opened up his scriptures. "Consider how much justice you want as I read this:

> And thus we see that all mankind were fallen, and they were in the grasp of justice; yea, the justice of God, which consigned them forever to be cut off from his presence.
>
> And now, the plan of mercy could not be brought about except an atonement should be made; therefore God himself atoneth for the sins of the world, to bring about the plan of mercy, to appease the demands of justice, that God might be a perfect, just God, and a merciful God also.

"Justice doesn't sound so good," Ken said as he looked over at Anna.

"Right," Anna said, not sounding completely convinced. "We all sin and need God's goodness."

"Do you want a guaranteed way to be sure God will be very forgiving of you on judgment day?" Bishop North asked as he turned the pages of his scriptures again. "The Lord spelled out in detail how we can receive as much forgiveness and mercy as we want on that day. It's in Matthew chapter 6." He read:

> For if ye forgive men their trespasses, your heavenly Father will also forgive you:
>
> But if ye forgive not men their trespasses, neither will your Father forgive your trespasses.

"So what is the formula?" Bishop North asked.

"Be very forgiving," Erica said, although her features expressed that her thoughts were far away.

"Exactly," Bishop North said. "Earlier in the Sermon on the Mount, Jesus said, 'Blessed are the merciful: for they shall obtain mercy.' "

"I need God's mercy. I want to forgive," Ken said, lifting his face out from his hands. "But I don't know how. I've tried, but I just don't know how to forgive. How do I do it?"

Bishop North looked at Erica and Anna. He could see that

they also held the same question and struggle as Ken. "We have learned a lot about grace over the last weeks, but there is not an aspect of grace that is more redeeming, more godly, than this type of grace. Here is the aspect of grace that changes lives more than any other: the grace to forgive. Jesus taught a parable about this type of forgiving grace," Bishop North said. "It's in Matthew 18. The parable begins with Peter asking Jesus how often his brother can offend him before he is no longer required to forgive him. Then before Jesus had a chance to answer, Peter offered the number seven as possibly the required total he would have to forgive. As you know, instead of agreeing with Peter, he says, 'seventy times seven.' So 490 is how many times we have to forgive, and after that we can refuse forgiveness?"

Ken smiled and shook his head.

"No, of course not," Bishop said, speaking the unspoken response from the group. "It's also a funny question since Peter's brother Andrew, who was one of the apostles, was probably standing right there when Peter asked the question. It could have been that Peter wanted Jesus to settle some family argument. Then Jesus goes on to teach the most incredible parable about forgiveness. He starts to tell of a king and a man who owed the king money. The man who was brought before the king owed the king ten thousand talents. Do you know about how much money a talent is today?"

"No idea," Anna replied.

"I learned that a talent wasn't just a regular coin. One talent of gold weighed between sixty to eighty pounds. Imagine," Bishop continued, "that much gold today. If gold today were about 700 hundred dollars an ounce, and there's sixteen ounces in a pound, times 60 pounds, and this guy owed ten thousand of these. . ."

"That's well over six billion dollars," Anna answered.

"That seems unbelievable," Ken commented.

"You're right. Sometimes politicians start throwing around the 'billion' word, and we don't even realize how much that really is. We can wrap our heads around how much a thousand dollars is, right? If I were to give you a thousand dollars every day, how many years would it take for me to pay you a billion dollars?"

"That would take close to 3,000 years," Anna responded.

"Yes," Bishop North smiled. "And this man in the parable owed more than six billion in today's money."

"It's not even possible for a single person to borrow—or ever pay back—that much money," Ken objected.

"Maybe you're right," Bishop North said. "But soon we'll see that there is a really good reason Jesus picked this incredibly large debt for the man to owe. Of course, the man couldn't pay the debt so then it says,

> But forasmuch as he had not to pay, his lord commanded him to be sold, and his wife, and children, and all that he had, and payment to be made.
>
> The servant therefore fell down, and worshipped him, saying, Lord, have patience with me, and I will pay thee all.
>
> Then the lord of that servant was moved with compassion, and loosed him, and forgave him the debt.

"The man said he would pay the debt but it would probably take hundreds of lifetimes to ever even earn a fraction of that much money. But the incredible thing is what the king did with the debt when the man pleaded for mercy. What does it mean in the verse when it says he 'forgave' the debt?"

"It was forgiven?" Anna questioned. "The debt was wiped clean? Banks don't do that today," Anna guffawed.

"They sure don't," Bishop North agreed. "No interest rate adjustments, no extended payment plans. Because of the king's graciousness, the debt was removed completely, without strings attached. Imagine if a family today wasn't able to pay their mortgage and the lending institution decided to just give them the house instead. That is what makes the next part of the story so strange."

Anna looked down again into Matthew 18.

> But the same servant went out, and found one of his fellowservants, which owed him an hundred pence: and he laid hands on him, and took him by the throat, saying, Pay me that thou owest.
>
> And his fellowservant fell down at his feet, and besought him, saying, Have patience with me, and I will pay thee all.
>
> And he would not: but went and cast him into prison, till he should pay the debt.

"Why is this man looking for the people who owed him

money now?" Bishop North asked, "To raise funds so he could pay the king back?"

"No," Ken replied. "That debt was completely forgiven. There was no debt to pay back."

"It's also interesting to look at how much one hundred pence is. Look at the footnote."

"Approximately three months' wages of a poor working man," Anna read from the bottom of the page.

"Today, if a poor working man works for eight dollars an hour, forty hours a week . . ." Anna again started to think through the numbers as Bishop North spoke.

"That would be a little over four thousand dollars," Erica answered.

"But, my friends," Bishop North started in again. "What does this have to do with forgiveness and how we should treat others?"

Ken thought for a minute. He started to think of what all the people represented in the parable. "The king represents God, and we are like the guy who owed all that money."

"What do the ten thousand talents represent?" Bishop North inquired further.

"We owe God a lot for all He has done for us," Erica said thoughtfully.

Bishop North smiled in agreement. "We are so indebted to the Lord. I guess you could say the ten thousand talents represent all of the mercy, care, love, blood, and effort the Lord has put into each one of us."

Anna thought for a moment. "So does that amount say what it cost the Lord to be able to forgive me of my sins?"

Instead of answering, Bishop North paused, letting the realization settle in. Then Bishop North started to quote part of a scripture he had learned years ago: Doctrine and Covenants 19:18.

> Which suffering caused myself, even God, the greatest of all, to tremble because of pain, and to bleed at every pore, and to suffer both body and spirit—and would that I might not drink the bitter cup, and shrink.

"It cost Jesus dearly to be able to forgive our sins. In fact," Bishop considered, "I don't even think six billion would be a close number if we had to put a monetary value on the effort of the

Atonement for each one of us. The scriptures use the term 'infinite atonement.' "

Anna mulled over what the scriptures were saying. "I never considered what it cost the Lord to be able to forgive me. I just thought forgiveness from God was like God had a magic wand, and He could just wave it and our sins would disappear."

Anna began to speak more slowly, and her voice caught on her words. "But instead of a magic wand, I now have this image of Jesus being crushed down in the agony and pains of my sins."

"It cost him dearly to be able to forgive each one of us," Bishop North added as he saw a tear rolling further down Anna's cheek, "So dearly. But this still doesn't conclude our topic about forgiveness. According to the parable, why should I forgive those who offend or hurt me?" he asked.

Ken again thought back on the parable and what the elements represented. "It has to do with the second man who owed the first man a hundred pence, doesn't it?"

"That's right. Why should the first man have forgiven the debt that the second man owed him?" Bishop asked.

"Because he had just been forgiven an incredible amount," Anna answered. "I guess when we understand how much the Lord has forgiven us, we should be quick to forgive others. Compared to what Jesus has forgiven of us, what others do to us could seem like nothing."

"But remember," Bishop reminded, "the second man owed quite a bit of money to the first. What if someone hurt you to the degree of four thousand dollars? Could you easily just let that go?"

"Although I still consider four thousand dollars a lot, there are still worse things," Ken said as he looked at the others. "A spouse who is unfaithful; being sexually abused by a stepparent; an accident that causes your child to become grossly handicapped. All of these cost far more than a few thousand dollars' worth of suffering."

"You are right," Bishop North said with a heavy look in his eyes. "In this life there is hurt far worse than what the second man in the parable owed the first. But even those things, as terrible as they are, are still a drop in the bucket compared to all the Lord has done for each of us. Here is the principle: The Lord will never ask you to forgive more than He forgives you. So we are to forgive all others, not because they are sorry or they have earned our forgiveness, but because of all that God has forgiven us. Just like in the parable."

"When we consider what the Lord has suffered for each of us," Ken said thoughtfully, "forgiving others seems more possible."

"And consider the implications when we decide not to forgive," Bishop North added. "If God forgives far more, at a greater cost, but we won't forgive lesser offenses, it is like we are 'one-upping' God. Imagine someone saying, 'God may forgive you, but I won't.' Who are we to hold someone's mistake over his or her head after all God has forgiven us? In Ephesians 4:32 it says:

> And be ye kind one to another, tenderhearted, forgiving one another, even as God for Christ's sake hath forgiven you.

"Notice that God is the standard of forgiveness. The Lord will never ask us to forgive more than He has forgiven us," he repeated.

"Forgiveness and letting everything go looks so inviting," Anna said in exasperation, "yet it seems so impossible. I know God has forgiven far more of us, but what about the pain of what others have done? How can we just let what they did go?" Anna questioned, looking at the others to see if they agreed.

"Do you know the story of Philemon?" Bishop North asked the group while opening his scriptures again. "Philemon is one of the books of the New Testament. The story here in Philemon might help. The book of Philemon is a letter that Paul wrote to his friend Philemon. Prior to the letter, Philemon had a bondservant named Onesimus. Today we might think of Onesimus as a slave, except he was a slave because of debts. This servant had run away, and tradition claims that he was caught and put into a prison in Rome where he met Paul. There Paul taught the runaway slave the gospel. As part of this man's repentance, he would need to return to his master. So this book is a letter Paul wrote to his friend Philemon, asking him to take back his runaway bondservant. In those times, a Roman could punish a runaway slave by having him put to death. But Paul, mediating for the man, says to his friend Philemon:

> If thou count me therefore a partner, receive him as myself.

> If he hath wronged thee, or oweth thee ought, put that on mine account.

"In other words, Paul is asking Philemon to show grace to his runaway servant. And Paul says that if Philemon feels like he has been wronged too greatly, he was to put that on Paul's account. This is a type, or an example, of how Christ is with us. The Lord wants us to show goodness and mercy toward all. Like Paul said, to show that grace to another is like showing it to the Lord himself. And if there is injustice, and if someone has got to pay a debt, the Savior says, 'Put it on my account. I'll repay the wrong to you. I'll make it right.'

"We live in a world of checks and balances," Bishop North went on. "Not just with money and governmental powers but in relationships. We measure what we do according to what others have done. We are always seeking a balance. We look at what others have done to us, and we often want to do accordingly to them. We look at what others deserve, merit, or have coming to them. And when we've been wronged, we want the debt repaid. That is what Paul is teaching here about God's grace. If we have been wronged by another, the Lord says we can put it on His account. The world pursues after and idealizes justice. Grace is about being unjust. When we think of injustice, we usually assume it means being less than fair: a person getting less than what he deserves, what he earned, or what is just. But grace startles everyone by giving more than what is fair, deserved, or merited. With grace, justice is met, surpassed, and then left far behind. Grace is about exceeding the demands of justice. Why? Because the Lord has bountifully exceeded all natural expectations in the way He has loved and looked after us and given us what we need.

"Like I said, the grace to forgive is greater than any form of grace that can be given," Bishop North continued. "Have you ever wanted to start over again? Often people consider divorce not just because of who the other person is, but because of what they have become. Through grace and forgiveness we can start fresh and allow others to start over again. 'But someone has to pay,' you might say. 'It isn't fair,' or 'They owe me.' 'How can I just let it go?' The answer is, you don't have to let it go. Someone has paid.

The Lord says to us, 'If someone has wronged you, put it on my account. If you've been wronged, let me take care of it.' In forgiving others, you can be free for the first time. The world is looking for someone to blame to feel better, but the Lord says, 'Forgive and be free.' The Lord will take care of it if there is vengeance to be paid. Leave it in His hands. He will take care of you and fill the empty places in your heart. It is because He has been so overwhelmingly good to you that you can afford to be incredibly good to others—to forgive anything."

chapter twenty-two

FULL

"Okay then," Ken said with resignation. "Like President Packer said to Elder Andersen, 'I'm nobody.' I guess that's true with me too then. I'm nobody," Ken repeated. "But I don't see how that will give me the strength to show grace like you are saying. I should forgive because the Lord has been generous in His forgiveness for me. I think I get your logic," Ken went on. "You think that by realizing that I'm no better than Deborah, I should be quick to forgive. By realizing God's forgiveness is greater, I should be able to forgive more easily. But I just don't feel that I can."

Ken looked around at the others, but there was no response. It felt to Ken like the times he was winning an argument in a court case, yet this was one he didn't want to win. Still, he didn't know what else to think. "Years ago I read a book by Dale Carnegie called *How to Win Friends and Influence People*. In the book were all these wonderful things to do that would win a bunch of friends and influence a lot of people. I tried doing all of the suggested strategies. In the book, the author said that if I would do things like smiling, calling people by their first names, showing genuine interest, thinking from their perspective, and other things, then I would be a success. I knew those things were true when I read them. They made sense to me. The problem was I didn't have it in me. He said to just do it, but it only worked for a short time. Soon, despite all the reminders and effort, I just didn't have anything left in me to give on that level of giving. I had poured out my strength in trying and was left empty.

"In the last few weeks, it's been the same with you," Ken went on. "You have wanted us to show tremendous grace and goodness toward others. But I don't have the strength. Like I said earlier, I'm empty, and I don't have anything there to give."

With the finality of Ken's words, Erica's and Anna's eyes shifted toward the ground as they considered what had been said and then looked up at Bishop North. Ken also looked to his bishop with the hope of some response. Bishop North gave them a thoughtful look and then closed his eyes, put his hands over his face, and breathed in deeply. As his hands came down, there was an expression of pain on his tired face.

"It's so hard to express my feelings about God's grace," Bishop North said, finally responding. "And I am such a weak messenger. Perhaps I've gone about teaching all of this in the wrong way. You are absolutely right, Ken. Grace asks us to give to others generously. But grace can't work on deficit spending for long."

"Deficit spending?" Ken questioned.

"Right," Bishop North said. "In the end, a person can't give what they haven't been given. You can't pour from an empty pitcher. In the long run, people can only give to the degree that they have been given. That is why lasting grace is not possible to give without the strength and Spirit the Lord Jesus Christ gives to us first. Once a person is broken of his pride, the Lord can heal that person. Once a person realizes that the world will always leave him empty in the end, the Lord can begin to fill that person. The Savior can then fill the empty places in our lives so that we might always have His Spirit to be with us.

"Of our own selves, we cannot give great goodness to others," Bishop North said. "We do not have that reservoir of goodness inside of us. But a follower of Christ can:

> Give more than he has been given,
> Love more than he has been loved,
> Care more than he has been cared for,
> Show kindness beyond the kindness he's been shown,
> Serve more than he has been served, and finally,
> Forgive more than he has been forgiven.

"But the follower of Christ can only do all these things for others because the Lord has done all these things for him—because the Lord has made up and will continue to make up for all the differences.

"Maybe I've been teaching this all wrong," Bishop North repeated. "I guess I've been focusing on giving grace. But you can't give grace until you have received grace. The scriptures give the best examples of this. For Isaiah, it wasn't until he was purged of his sins that he eagerly responded to the Lord's call to share His word with others. He first received the light before he was excited to share the light with others. Likewise, it wasn't until Enos prayed and received a forgiveness of his own sins that he then prayed for the Nephites and then the Lamanites. Alma and the four sons of King Mosiah were awful people, going around trying to destroy the Church. But after they experienced the Lord's goodness, they wanted to spend the rest of their lives sharing God's goodness with others. It's the same story with Saul, who later became the Apostle Paul. We have to receive grace first before we are able to share that grace with others."

"Wait," Ken said. "I don't think I have this reservoir of the Lord's goodness, but I've been baptized. I've been given the gift of the Holy Ghost. I take the sacrament each week. Why don't I feel this strength you are talking about?"

"You've participated in all of these ordinances outwardly," Bishop North said. "But what about inwardly? When was the last time that you really felt these things in your heart? When was the last time you pled for the Lord's forgiveness and felt that cleansing power in your soul? When was the last time you really surrendered yourself to God's will in your life? We don't believe that being forgiven by the Lord and committing ourselves to Him are one-time events. We constantly need these things. Go to the Lord and express your nothingness; surrender yourself; commit yourself. Plead for His grace, and you will receive it. It's only after you have received His goodness that you will be able to give that goodness to others. You have to receive grace to give grace."

chapter twenty-three

THE WORKS OF GRACE

Ken sat in his car outside his house and thought about all that Bishop North had said. He opened up the glove box and found a Book of Mormon he had put in there years earlier. Although the book was dusty and dirty on the outside, the pages were all white inside. He turned to Alma 22. In verse 15 he read:

> And it came to pass that after Aaron had expounded these things unto him, the king said: What shall I do that I may have this eternal life of which thou hast spoken? Yea, what shall I do that I may be born of God, having this wicked spirit rooted out of my breast, and receive his Spirit, that I may be filled with joy, that I may not be cast off at the last day? Behold, said he, I will give up all that I possess, yea, I will forsake my kingdom, that I may receive this great joy.

Ken thought about how similar the king's feelings were to his own. He read on.

> But Aaron said unto him: If thou desirest this thing, if thou wilt bow down before God, yea, if thou wilt repent of all thy sins, and will bow down before God, and call on his name in faith, believing that ye shall receive, then shalt thou receive the hope which thou desirest.

"I want to be a new person also, Lord," he prayed. "Please forgive me of all of my shortcomings. Help me to change. I know I'm nothing of myself. And without thy mercy and grace, Lord, my life will fall apart completely. Please help me as I go in and talk to Deborah. Please heal our marriage. Help me to forgive completely and heal our family."

As Ken went through his front door, he realized that he had no idea what he would say or do. He felt like Nephi going into Jerusalem to get the brass plates; he was simply being led by the Spirit, not knowing beforehand what he would do.

Ken expected to find his wife in their bedroom, but he didn't see her. He felt a pinch in his stomach as he thought she might be in their walk-in closet again. He remembered how he had last seen her there with his gun, ready to take her own life. Ken took a deep breath, walked in the closet, and turned on the light. Deborah wasn't in there either, but as he turned to leave, he noticed a row of scrapbooks Deborah had carefully compiled over the years for their family. Ken sat down and started to look through the scrapbooks. He was impressed by the careful attention to detail and the love that went into these books. New guilt swept over him as he realized he had never given more than a glance at these books before now. With each page he saw the many wonderful times they'd had over the years. Then he looked to the most recent book and saw that it had last been updated just before Jimmy's accident. Ken thought back on that fateful night that he had tried so hard to block out in his mind. He thought about how he had come home late. "If I had been home earlier, would none of this have happened?" Then he realized his wife had never said a word of blame to him.

The last page of the scrapbook was a white piece of cardboard made to protect the scrapbook pages. On that white cardboard he imagined the picture of his son in the water that had been taken only in Ken's mind. But instead of feeling bad for his son, his mind dwelled on the feelings his wife must have been feeling for all of these months. He thought of how her thoughts must have been similar to his. How she mourned for her son almost like he had died because the life he was going to have had died with the accident.

Deborah jumped a bit as she walked into the closet and saw Ken there. "Wait!" Ken said as she quickly turned back out to leave. "Please don't go."

Deborah stopped there in the archway of the closet. Ken knew he had just a moment before she would continue walking. "I'm so sorry, Deborah. As if it wasn't enough hurt to have the accident, I've made everything worse by the way I've treated you. I haven't been there for you. And I've blamed you when it wasn't your—or anyone's—fault."

Deborah didn't move as Ken stared at her shoulders. "Please forgive me for the way I've been treating you," Ken said as he put the scrapbook down, stood up, and moved closer to his wife. "Please let me have a chance to change and be the man I should be. Please, Deborah. I love you."

"Did you feel forced into this," Deborah asked, "with the whole gun thing? Forced love isn't love at all."

Ken wanted to lie, but he knew she would know it was a lie. "I saw yesterday that your life was at rock bottom like I felt mine was. I started to think about everything and how much I had to lose. I love you, Deborah. I love all that we were. I saw how I've neglected you over these years."

"What about all of your talks with the bishop?" Deborah said without turning around.

"He's been teaching me about God's grace. He's been teaching me that we all need His grace, so who are we to hurt or blame another?"

"But what happened is my fault," Deborah pointed out without emotion.

"No, Deborah," Ken said. "It's not. It was an awful accident in this fallen world. God wants to offer us a new and better life, but we have to forgive each other. I want to live with that mighty change of heart, Deborah. If there is anything I need to forgive, then I forgive you with all of my heart. Will you also forgive me?"

Anna opened Joyce's scriptures. Anna had taken Caitlin with her and decided to stay at her sister's home. She had been thinking about King Benjamin telling his people of their nothingness. As she tried to find the place in Mosiah, she stumbled upon a different verse. In the beginning of chapter 4 it said:

> And they had viewed themselves in their own carnal state, even less than the dust of the earth. And they all cried aloud with

> one voice, saying: O have mercy, and apply the atoning blood of Christ that we may receive forgiveness of our sins, and our hearts may be purified; for we believe in Jesus Christ, the Son of God, who created heaven and earth, and all things; who shall come down among the children of men.
>
> And it came to pass that after they had spoken these words the Spirit of the Lord came upon them, and they were filled with joy, having received a remission of their sins, and having peace of conscience, because of the exceeding faith which they had in Jesus Christ who should come, according to the words which king Benjamin had spoken unto them.

She turned the page to chapter 5 and read:

> And they all cried with one voice, saying: Yea, we believe all the words which thou hast spoken unto us; and also, we know of their surety and truth, because of the Spirit of the Lord Omnipotent, which has wrought a mighty change in us, or in our hearts, that we have no more disposition to do evil, but to do good continually.

Then Anna turned to Alma chapter 5. She looked down at verse 14, which her sister had marked.

> And now behold, I ask of you, my brethren of the church, have ye spiritually been born of God? Have ye received his image in your countenances? Have ye experienced this mighty change in your hearts?

Anna thought back on the last week and a half and the feelings she had experienced. She thought of how she had felt God's goodness and how the Lord had started to renew her as a person. She loved that she had become excited about life, was becoming a new person, and saw potential in their marriage. Then she thought about how Mitch's revelation had changed everything. Since then Anna's world seemed crushed.

On the other side of the page she saw another verse that had been marked.

> And now behold, I say unto you, my brethren, if ye have experienced a change of heart, and if ye have felt to sing the song of redeeming love, I would ask, can ye feel so now?

I want to, Lord, Anna thought. *I really do.*

"Where are you headed?" Joyce asked when Anna stood up.

"Joyce, could you watch Caitlin for me?" Anna asked. "I need to try something."

"Absolutely," Joyce said as she looked deeply into her sister's eyes.

"I want to try to talk with Mitch."

"I'll keep praying for you two," Joyce said as Anna left.

A few minutes later, Anna was at her apartment.

"Hello, Anna," Mitch said as she entered. He bit down on his lip, having no idea what Anna was feeling.

"Mitch," Anna finally said after hanging up her coat and sliding down against a wall into a sitting position. "I want to feel different. Last week I felt a glimpse of what we could be and the person I want to be. I want those things so badly, but I don't think you understand how much those things you have done have hurt me and Caitlin. I've wondered if I can ever trust you again."

"I will earn your trust again," Mitch said. "I also want everything we started to have last week again. Last night I was so discouraged. I felt like I had ruined everything and there was no hope. Then temptation came again with the computer, but I didn't give in. I hate what I have become. I got so angry at what I had done, and potentially ruined, that I wanted to toss my computer out the window. I'm determined to do whatever it takes. I'm so determined never to look at pornography again; we'll set you up as the administrator on our computers. We'll install filter software. And after that, if I ever mess up again, there will be no computer at all for me."

"What about the woman at work?" Anna asked.

"I don't have any feelings for her. I'll never talk with her again except when I have to for business purposes," Mitch said. "I'll avoid even getting near her. If it will help, I'll even put in for a transfer on Monday. Whatever you think."

"It isn't about what I think!" Anna burst out in tears. "It's about what you think and think about. I want love, not lust. I want your heart."

"You have it," Mitch said softly after moving over and sitting next to Anna. "Like you, I want to be a different person.

"There's something else," Mitch said. "I've been really bad about something. I haven't been very good at saying I'm sorry. I've always thought that if I just showed I was sorry, that was better. But I haven't even done well at that. But Anna, I'm so sorry. Please forgive me."

Anna could hear his voice choking and that he was in tears too. A thought ran through her head about letting him suffer a bit and pay for what he had done. Hold it over his head for a few days. But then Anna thought about God's grace and how she was trying not to keep score anymore. She wanted to show grace in the same way God had with her.

"I need to say something too," Anna said after minutes of sitting there in silence. "I've been thinking back. Over the years, I think there were a lot of times that I was angry at you, but I was the one who was causing my own unhappiness."

"Wait," Mitch said. "I've hardly been a good husband."

"Maybe that's true," Anna said. "But that's not the point. Often when I was not being what I should be, I would not take personal responsibility for the things I was doing that were making me unhappy. Maybe to protect my pride, I would try to find others to blame and often it was you. Lately I've realized that I can never become the person I want to be unless I stop trying to find others to blame and take responsibility for myself. Finding others to blame has never made me happy. It's only fed my pride, which has always made me feel down."

"Let's forget everything in the past then," Mitch said. "Let's start afresh and as new people. Will you let me?"

"Let's do it together," Anna said as she slipped her hand into his.

"Please come in," said the counselor from the Department of Family Services who was assigned to Erica's case years ago. "Sorry for the mess. It's been at least a year since I've seen you and we've talked. How are you doing?"

"I've been okay," Erica said with a subtle forced smile as she sat down.

"It's been a crazy week. I only got to review your court case again a few minutes ago. I guess you got the letter stating that Dean will be getting out and that he will be placed in a halfway house. But you also understand that he will have a restraining order. He will not be allowed to come near you."

"I understand all of the terms," Erica said.

"Then why did you want to come and see me?" the counselor asked. "Is there anything I can do for you? Do you need to talk?"

"I want you to get this letter to Dean," Erica said as she handed an envelope over to the counselor.

"You understand I need to review this."

"Go ahead and read it," Erica said, briefly smiling her consent. "It's okay."

The counselor eyed Erica, wondering about her motivation, and then opened the unsealed envelope.

Dean,

I'm writing you this letter to let you know I forgive you for the awful things you did to me.

This forgiveness does not come easily. Your actions have caused me unspeakable suffering. But I have learned about God's great love and grace toward me. He has shown me goodness far beyond anything I deserve. And through God's goodness, He expects me to forgive all those who have hurt me. As I have been working on forgiving you, I have felt freedom. I feel I am no longer chained to the memories of the hurt you caused me. I have felt God's healing power.

Naturally, you will understand that I do not want any contact with you and if you should break the restraining order, I will inform the authorities immediately. It is best if our lives are completely separate. Just because I have forgiven you, it does not mean I trust you. Forgiveness is given, but trust is earned. And because the things you did were so wrong, I will not allow you an opportunity to earn my trust again. Like I said, we must have no contact, and I'll leave anything further for God and the next life.

I wish you the best and pray that God can also change you and show His great goodness to you. If there is any further vengeance to be given out for what you have done, I'll leave it to God to repay. I'm now free.

Erica

"Wow," the counselor said as he now studied Erica. "You're

not the same girl I counseled with for months."

"I guess not," Erica said as she started to stand up. "I'll go ahead and leave you to all the work you have."

"Wait," the counselor said. "I don't understand how you have gotten to this point. Are you *really* doing well? You were so full of anger and resentment before. What's happened to bring about this change?"

"I'm not sure you'll fully understand," Erica said. "It's really different than the way we talked. I found something that's helped me that you never talked to me about."

"What's that?"

"You showed me that I was not to blame and that what Dean did was the source of my problems. I appreciate that," Erica said. "We talked a lot, but all I learned then was to blame him for my hurt. But that blame never healed me."

"Then a friend showed me about God's grace and how I needed to forgive to be healed," Erica went on. "God wants me to forgive and show grace toward Dean, not because he deserves it or has earned it, but because God has been so good to me. I have learned of and felt God's goodness toward me, and now He expects me to show that same goodness toward everyone else. The Lord has taught me how to feel again. God has shown me that by forgiving, I can be free from the memories that have controlled me and hurt me. Like I said, God has set me free."

epilogue

NEW LIFE

Grace changed everything, but not all at once. Over the next few years, Bishop North saw a great change in these individuals.

Ken showed greater and more deliberate love toward Deborah than he had ever shown before in their marriage. Slowly grace—and the Lord's Spirit—thawed the cold places in Deborah's heart. This spread to the whole family. Although Jimmy's condition never changed completely, he became happier too. There was also a new faith that grew in their family as they looked forward to the resurrection, when the Savior would make Jimmy whole again. Through the coming years, the two of them became deeply involved in community charity work. Perhaps this is because once someone experiences God's goodness, they want to show that goodness toward others. Five years later, Ken replaced Stewart North as the bishop.

Erica's life also changed. She stopped attending Bishop North's ward and joined the Young Single Adult branch and the institute class in the area. There she met a wonderful returned missionary who later took her to the temple. The Lord had healed the wounds she had received in life. She now lives her life after the manner of happiness.

Anna and Mitch also saw the Lord revive their marriage. The two occasionally ran into difficulties, but they had the tools to take on those challenges. They understood that they both needed the Lord's goodness. They also understood that they always needed to be good to each other and not give according to what they felt they had been given. It wasn't always easy, but as they each showed grace, they felt the love of the Savior more and the grace He constantly extended to them. The two got off of the sidelines in the ward and served the Lord deliberately. Anna and Mitch also had four more children together and brought them up in a pleasing way to the Lord. Joy had replaced the pain and misery of their marriage.

A year after the great change in their marriage, Mitch and Anna were at the temple with their ward and were doing sealings. During a spare moment, Anna noticed that she was seated before mirrors that were similar to the ones she had looked into a year earlier. But now she saw the reflections differently. Before she thought of the repeating reflections representing the uncertainty of her future. But now she saw the exact opposite. Rather than seeing those repeated hazy images being her future, she saw them as the past. Rather than trying to see where the images began, she saw who she was at that moment. She saw past years making her into the person she was now. And she liked who she now saw. She could feel a future of becoming the person God wanted her to become. And what made it all the more wonderful was that she had her husband again in that reflection of the mirrors. As she looked into those mirrors, she felt an excitement to continue on together and experience all that God had for them as a family.

Through the Savior, Anna, Ken, and Erica saw their lives change, which then changed the lives of everyone around them. But more than anything, they saw the Savior differently: more magnificent than they had ever imagined, with a grace and love that didn't make sense—an impractical grace. And that is what makes it all the more wonderful.

discussion questions

1. Have you ever had an unexpected event that suddenly changed everything in life? What was it?
2. How does marriage relate to personal growth? When can marriage and growth be independent of each other?
3. Are there some experiences that seem too hard to overcome? Experiences too hard to forgive?
4. Have you ever tried to help someone who had given up on God? How?
5. When have you experienced grace from someone? When have you experienced God's grace?
6. How does love become conditional in many marriages?
7. Have you ever considered keeping the commandments as a way to get what you want from God? What is wrong with this point of view?
8. How has goodness from another person changed you? When you gave grace to another, what effect did it have on the other person? What effect did it have on you?
9. Have you ever expected another person to make you happy? Why doesn't this work in the long run?
10. How is love an action rather than a static feeling?
11. What do good works show our Heavenly Father?

12. What role does opposition play in our possible progression? What role is the Atonement supposed to play in our trials?
13. Why are we tempted to keep score in our relationships? Why are people often hesitant to give more than is deserved?
14. What are some ways you have been gracious to your spouse or others? How can practicing what to do in a situation be helpful?
15. How is it that we are never out of God's reach to save?
16. What part do pride and humility play in happiness?
17. How does the world determine your worth? How does God determine it? Which do you pay the most attention to?
18. Why is forgiving so difficult? What has helped you learn to forgive?
19. What role does justice play in forgiveness? How is justice one of the greatest forms of grace?
20. How does accepting personal responsibility help bring about change?

about the author

John S. Bushman is proud to be the father of five, the son of two, and the husband of one. He grew up in Tempe, Arizona, and served a mission in the Philippines. Later he got his bachelor's degree in psychology and his master's in instructional technology from ASU.

For the last ten years, he has worked as a full-time seminary instructor for the Church's seminaries and institutes in St. George, Utah. Now he teaches institute and coordinates the seminary program in northwest Washington. Second to the Lord and his family, his greatest love is teaching and studying the scriptures with the youth of the Church.

One of his other passions is writing. He has been writing for the last few years, and he and some friends have recently published three books with Deseret Book: *Scripture Study for Latter-day Saint Families—The Book of Mormon* and two similar volumes for the Doctrine and Covenants and the New Testament.